Autonomy and Obedience
in the Catholic Church

Autonomy and Obedience in the Catholic Church

The Future of Catholic Moral Leadership

QUENTIN DE LA BÉDOYÈRE

T & T CLARK
A Continuum imprint
LONDON • NEW YORK

T&T CLARK LTD

A Continuum imprint

The Tower Building   370 Lexington Avenue
11 York Road   New York 10017–6503
London SE1 7NX, UK   USA

www.continuumbooks.com

British Library Cataloguing-in-Publication Data

A catalogue record for this book is available from the British Library
ISBN 0 567 08852 9 (Paperback)
ISBN 0 567 08906 1 (Hardback)

Revised Standard Version of the Bible, copyright 1952 by the Division of Christian Education of the National Council of the Churches of Christ in the United States of America. Used by permission. All rights reserved.

The author thanks the following for permission to quote from their publications:
Catholic Truth Society, 40–46 Harleyford Road, London, SE11 5AY
Geoffrey Chapman (for *The Documents of Vatican II*, edited by Walter M Abbott, SJ, 1996)

Typeset by Fakenham Photosetting Ltd, Fakenham, Norfolk NR21 8NN
Printed and bound in Great Britain by Bookcraft, Midsomer Norton

In memory of my father, Michael de la Bédoyère, who devoted his life to the participation of the laity in the good of the Church

CONTENTS

ACKNOWLEDGEMENTS

This book was triggered by a paper I was invited to give to the Newman Association in Wimbledon, and I am grateful for their inspiration and the questions they asked.

My particular thanks go to Gordon Heald and Michael Hornsby-Smith for checking and confirming that I have not misquoted their general drift in Chapter 1, and also to Andrew Greeley for his valuable website on Catholic sociology, although I was unable to make contact with him directly. I trust I have not misinterpreted his reports.

Similarly, I owe a debt to Catholic Pages, the Catholic Information Network and the Fathers of the English Dominican Province who have provided me with invaluable research through the internet. I would also acknowledge New Advent's powerful contribution to the dissemination of Catholic documents. Among others I found their transcription of the 1913 Catholic Encyclopaedia an almost daily companion.

I am indebted to the library at Heythrop College, and therefore to Michael Walsh, for the use of their facilities.

Professor John Marshall reviewed the text and gave me some much valued comments; naturally, any errors remain my responsibility.

As always, my particular thanks go to my wife, Irené, who used a painstaking pencil to point up obscure passages and infelicitous expressions. And I have benefited greatly from discussion with her of various issues – though the views expressed remain my own.

INTRODUCTION

In 1966 I wrote an article in the Jesuit periodical *The Month* under the title of 'The Responsible Conscience'. My starting point was that the comprehensive network of moral instruction proposed by the Church with varying degrees of authority created a climate in which moral decision was primarily a matter of obedience. What was the point of employing an active conscience if the answers were in the back of the book?

I traced a growing movement in theological circles, of some forty years standing, towards a return to the traditional and evangelical emphasis of love as the source and the end of the moral life. This, I argued, changed the focus from an arid legalism towards the fundamental question: what does love of God and man call me to in this decision? This presented a challenge to respond to Jesus' call that we should be perfect as opposed to resting on the supposed security of minimalist obedience.

This response required of its nature a fully active and autonomous conscience. It had to operate through our personal discernment of the divine law and its application to the particular circumstances. In other words it had to be formed. Of course it needed all the help it could get, and a major factor in that help was the teaching authority of the Church. But following the Church was not in itself sufficient. Even in infallible matters I remained responsible for accepting the authority of the Church as the instrument of God; in fallible matters I remained responsible either because I had verified the instruction for myself or because I believed in my uncertainty that the Church was the most likely source of the truth. But I could not hide behind her skirts on the Day of Judgement – on that day I and my conscience would stand naked before the Throne.

Much water in many streams has flowed under the bridge since then. The documents of the Second Vatican Council (completed the year before) began to bite. They gave clear support to the responsible conscience, while reaffirming the Church's authority; they became the deeds of manumission from the legalistic model of the Church which had been predominant for several centuries. Hard on their heels came the decision of *Humanae Vitae* (1968), extending the existing condemnation of artificial contraception to the reservation of fertility using the Pill. This was the crunch because it triggered a major conflict between definitive, but not infallible, moral teaching and the consciences of many clerics and in all levels of the laity. It was a historical watershed because for the first time the general Catholic community was faced by the solemn reiteration of a formal moral teaching which many had come to doubt – and acting on that doubt did not exclude them from the Church.

Since then there has been much progress – or regress, depending on your point of view. An influential trend in moral theology at high levels has continued to develop the ramifications of the autonomous conscience in a liberal direction basing the case on Scripture, Tradition, the Council and reason. Another school has stoutly defended the more conservative direction basing the case on Scripture, Tradition, the Council and reason. The first school had all the best tunes but was not necessarily singing from the right song sheet. In 1993 the Pope published to his fellow bishops his encyclical *Veritatis Splendor*;[1] it was occasioned by his wish to correct what he saw as false tendencies among some moral theologians of the liberal school, but he took the opportunity to survey the broad field of moral theology and in doing so to mark the boundaries of the orthodox.

The encyclical is a major element in a centralizing tendency in the Church which has occurred over this period. And the effects of this tendency have been felt throughout the structure of the Church. Although the Council had reaffirmed the independent local authority of the bishops and the importance of their collegiality in communion with the Pope, it seemed to many that the Holy See, through numerous Papal teachings, Curial instructions and censorship of 'rogue' theologians, the appointment of conservative bishops in 'difficult' countries, the encouragement of conservative movements such as Opus Dei and discouragement of liberal movements, was intent on governing the Church directly and down to its lowest levels. The Oath of Fidelity, previously required only of bishops, was extended to all who held office in the Church, and the Profession of Faith, required of such people, clarified.[2] The desire to bind the consciences of the faithful in sexual matters was no more than a symptom – important though it proved to be – of a much broader strategy to weld the Church into a community through centralized micro management. The legalist model of the Church, threatened by the Council, was being restored. The language had become emollient, persuasion rather than diktat was employed, but the direction was clear.

It is hard to judge whether this strategy has been successful since there are no generally agreed criteria. But should one adopt such pedestrian measurements as growth in membership, use of the Sacraments, increasing acceptance of the Church's authority and a healthy growing priesthood, one has to say, at least as far as Western countries are concerned, that it has not. In Chapter 1 I give an overview of the major measurable changes of recent years. Every tightening of the screw appears to have led to a greater alienation. One is forced to ask whether there might be a better way.

Ironically one ray of hope, challenge and opportunity emerged from *Humanae Vitae*. Just as the ruling was the first public moral conflict following the Council so it was the first occasion following the Council when its explicit endorsement of the radical freedom of conscience was put to practical test. A number of national hierarchies, while supporting the ruling, reminded their communities of this with various levels of qualification up to a clear statement that a properly formed conscience had to be followed even if it rejected the teaching. No such *caveat* appeared in the encyclical. For a moment it looked as if the Council's teaching was about to be taken seriously by the hierarchy, or at least by influential elements of it.

But the moment was lost. Instead of developing a practical programme for educating the community at all levels in the true formation of conscience, there has been effectively nothing, except good but general statements on the doctrine of conscience. The vacuum remained unfilled and today too many Catholics, in so far as they consider the matter at all, think that the forming of conscience is little more than consulting their own preferences. The Church has lost what authority it retained for its legalistic system and failed to give the leadership which could have replaced and enhanced its moral authority both within its own communion and in the world outside.

There are reasons why this happened which I shall discuss in due course but, more importantly, I want to look at the autonomy of the individual through a model for conscience formation which is entirely in accord with reason and Tradition, yet takes into account the practical insights which the secular world is able to offer. And this must be preceded by considering our personal formation – becoming the sort of person we ought to be in order to invoke conscience truly. The model will only be valuable if it provides a guide at the level of the individual and, moreover, if it can be practically incorporated into the schools and amongst adults, and its spirit is reflected in the activities and pronouncements of the Magisterium. This is a tall order but I am an optimist. However, the development of the autonomous conscience can only take place within a Church which practises autonomy throughout its own organization. There is an antithesis between the approach which holds that freedom should only be *curtailed* when there is sufficiently strong reason and an approach which holds that freedom should only be *allowed* where there is sufficiently strong reason.

My optimism is bolstered by other insights from the secular world. I want to show how the understanding of effective leadership and the exercise of authority radically altered during the twentieth century, and what the Church can learn from this. I argue that it is the way to go forward, converting the legal model into one more suited to a community of love – and so restoring the flickering pilot light of today's Church to its full flame. In essence my theme is that, through the right forms of leadership, it is possible to promote Christian autonomy at all levels from layman to archbishop without losing one jot or tittle of the Church's divine authority; on the contrary, secular experience indicates that it would enhance it. It is not an easy option but the evidence in its support is strong.

Some readers may think that it is an impertinence for a lay person untrained in the science of moral theology to attempt a contribution to this task. Sometimes I wonder about this myself. But I draw strength from the insistence of the Council[3] and other documents that lay people should be making such contributions provided they do so loyally, thoughtfully and responsibly. They can and should bring to bear experiences and resulting insights which in the nature of the case theological professionals are less likely to have. I bring to bear many years of former experience as a marriage counsellor in helping people to form their consciences, and an even longer period in industry both in chief executive and management consultancy roles. I have written widely about both counselling and management, and the interesting overlap which occurs between two such apparently disparate fields. Where my theological knowledge is concerned let me illustrate the point with a story which is the first, but will not be the last, in this book.

Most of my career took place on the marketing side of the life assurance industry. There the actuary with the million dollar brain and hard-won qualifications is king. Not only does he know the answers but also he provides a political safety net; no one gets sacked for taking the actuary's advice.

In the fullness of time I found that I had a team of actuaries working for me. And I wanted to understand what they were doing and why. This was apparently impossible because without several years of study and an artificial boost to my brainpower I could not be expected to grasp the issues. All I could do was to interfere. So I interfered by announcing that I would not accept any actuarial decision I did not understand.

Recognizing my intransigence they began to explain to me the basics of what they were doing and to put into infant language the reasons for their proposals. They did it extremely well, which was not surprising because they are intelligent people. Nor was I surprised that I could grasp issues without difficulty – there are few things from the actuarial science to the Theory of Relativity which cannot be understood by the lay mind when they are explained well. I even had the impression that the process of translation was enabling them to understand their own principles in a fuller way.

More pertinently, my questions and comments which arose from my different experience seemed to be making a difference. Without doubt the quality of their work and their proposals improved. My lay input helped them to be better actuaries.

I do not want to push the analogy too far. I have explained the basis for my temerity and I must leave judgements of its results to others. What effect will they have? At the time of my pipsqueak contribution in 1966 great theologians were following a similar theme (as they do today), and no one listened to them. If they had, the history of the subsequent forty years might have been very different. But the Church does not measure in brief instances of forty years: there is plenty of time to come. But we might remember that the time to come starts today.

I have included important references in my chapter endnotes. And I have given Internet addresses where they may be helpful. I hope this will provide for some easier access to the fuller context where this is needed.

My endnotes also include additional comments and examples where these have not sat conveniently in the main text. So please regard the endnotes as part of the book.

Although the term 'Magisterium' is relatively modern I have used it for convenience throughout as a shorthand for the Church's hierarchical teaching office. It enables me to distinguish between official proclamation of doctrine and the belief of the Church as a whole community. Although the first has the office of witness to the second they are not necessarily identical – either now or historically.

Finally, I hope I will be forgiven for ordinarily using the masculine, being gender-specific only where this is relevant. This is for eugraphic reasons, and I do not want to insult my readers by supposing they are unable to make the transposition.

Notes to Introduction

1. John Paul II's main documents (and other Papal documents) can be most easily found on the Internet by looking up the pope's

name on a good search engine. I use Google. There are several sources.

2. John Paul II, *Ad Tuendam Fidem* (28 May 1998) and Congregation for the Doctrine of the Faith (1 March 1989).

3. *De Ecclesia* 37.

CHAPTER 1

THE TROUBLED CHURCH

The Church of God is in trouble. Of course it has always been in trouble, in its internal dissension and in its external relations. This is bound to be – partly because it is a human institution and humans are imperfect, and partly because it is a divine institution bearing witness to God's word in a world which is not prone to receive it. Fortunately we have a guarantee that it will survive and that all manner of things will be well.

Today's problem has its own characteristics. There is a large and growing gap between the Church as a moral authority and its members. The gap is unusual because disaffection is explicit and so widespread. It occurs at all levels from its ordinary and active members to many of its theologians and of its own clergy. It is no longer good manners to ask a cleric his opinion on some moral matter for fear of putting him into an embarrassing position.

The Church engages directly with the world in many ways – for example, through national and international charity work, education, healthcare and hospitals, and social programmes such as the Campaign for Human Development in the USA. But it does not engage as a moral authority where it is seen as largely irrelevant, trapped in the amber of the past. Even aspects of its social work can be contaminated in secular eyes by aspects of its doctrines, particularly in developing countries where it may, in some respects, be seen as inhibiting programmes through its moral imperatives. The great social encyclicals such as *Mater et Magistra* and *Pacem in Terris*[1] live in the shadows – influencing, for those who read them, by their internal argument rather than by the authority of their sponsor.

The Statistics of Decline

The internal decline can be measured with depressing clarity. Gordon Heald in a report in the *Tablet*,[2] based on statistics taken from the 1999 *Catholic Directory* for England and Wales, demonstrates a clear pattern: between 1964 and 1997, baptisms declined by 49 per cent, confirmations by 48 per cent, first communions by 40 per cent, marriages by 68 per cent (though some of this may be accounted for by such factors as later age of marriage), Mass attendance by 48 per cent. In 1964 there was one priest to about 500 Catholic population; by 1997 this figure had increased to 700. Ordinations dropped by 48 per cent between 1964 and 1996. Although the level has remained steady for several years and shown a slow increase in the 1990s 'the number of new priests is still below the renewal rate of retiring or dying priests or those priests who have left the Church'. Conversions have remained steady, although, taking into account the movement of Anglicans resulting from the Church of England's acceptance of women priests, Heald suggests that 'without the Anglican converts the Catholic Church would not be receiving any converts today'. Of the measures he examines the only (but important) success is Catholic schools which, like other denominational schools, are popular with parents since they perform well educationally and teach Christian values seen as lacking in the secular state system.

Heald reports that this rapid decline is reflected throughout Europe. Although he notes that the Church is rapidly growing in Africa and Asia, he concludes: 'This is no excuse for not facing the facts, however. Without some reform the downward path will continue.'

Father Andrew Greeley, the sociologist, writing in and about the United States, uses a statistical method which measures changes in attitude of Catholics born at different times in the twentieth century but surveyed at the same age, thus eliminating the effects of life experience on religious attitudes and behaviour. His source is twenty-five years of records from the General Social Survey. He notes some plus points: that Catholics have maintained the same proportion of the population (some 25 per cent), that the defection rate (excluding Hispanics) has remained constant at 12 per cent, that belief in life after death has increased by 35 per cent between different generations measured at the same age, that by a similar measurement belief in God as compassionate has increased by 22 per cent.

On the other hand regular Mass attendance across generations has fallen from 62 per cent to about half, and there is a similar decline in daily prayer. Significantly 45 per cent of earlier generations expressed 'a very great deal of confidence in Church leaders'. In later generations this has dropped to 26 per cent. Around half of the earlier generations believed that premarital sex was always wrong; in the later generations this had dropped to 7 per cent.[3]

In 1965 there were 50,000 seminarians in training in the USA; by 1997 it had dropped to a tenth of that number. The average age of diocesan priests in 1999 was 58, and 25 per cent were over 70. For every 100 priests who died or resigned in Italy there were 50 to take their place; in Spain it was 35, Germany 34 , France 17 and Portugal 10.[4]

The shareholders of any public corporation which reported equivalent decline in measurable results would have considerable concerns about management performance long before this. The Church has only one shareholder, and he has undertaken that he will never sell his share. He has also promised permanent support for the authority of its office holders. All the greater reason then for the vicarious powers-that-be to accept with whole hearts that they are presiding over crisis. The reason of course might be that fidelity to her mission has necessarily made the Church unpopular with an evil and adulterous generation. But it would be safer to assume, as a working hypothesis, that leadership has failed to adapt to a quickly changing situation. The two possibilities are not, of course, incompatible.

Explanations

Many would argue that these alarming declines have been caused by a general loss of identity and a weak-kneed collusion in the so-called progressive attitudes of general society. The wind has been tempered to the shorn lamb, but the shorn lamb preferred no wind at all.

There has clearly been a loss in the signs of identity. The removal of Latin from the liturgy, for instance; or the relaxation of Friday abstinence. The general movement towards ecumenism at local, national and ecclesiastical levels has blurred the boundaries of the community. Despite the Church putting cautionary limits to certain aspects we have come a long way from the spirit epitomized a generation ago by a friend of mine: 'There's no problem about Ecumenism – they've only got to join us and the job's done.'

The loss of such signs should not be minimized. Communities have always defined themselves by something of this order. A community cannot exist without some maintenance of distinctive characteristics, and these are boundaries that can be clearly seen. The Jewish religion has traditionally used the observance of the Sabbath as one of its defining marks. 'Its strict observance was the mark of the pious Jew and distinguished him amid his pagan surroundings.'[5] One would expect a loss of community feeling and consequently of observance of community mores as a result, unless some equally effective substitute could be found.

There is evidence that an uncompromising stand on tough doctrines attracts many people.

Many years ago a friend of mine in the Anglican clergy became a Catholic. The reason he gave me was that he had been in the habit of consulting Catholic moral theologies for answers to pastoral questions. 'My lot not only didn't have the answers but they all disagreed – useless!' Eventually he decided, at considerable personal sacrifice, that he should convert. If we were still in touch I think it would be tactless to ask him how he feels now.

Islam, known for the firmness of its demanding moral doctrines, is now the second largest religion, at 1.35 billion. At its current growth rate of 3 per cent a year it will double in twenty-five years and at some point in the twenty-first century is expected to overtake Christianity (currently 1.95 billion). On a smaller scale, demanding sects both within and outside Christianity are generally flourishing. A good example is the Vineyard association of churches – a bright-eyed, Bible-based movement which, between 1985 and 2000, has established itself in over 70 countries. Apocalyptic and esoteric cults are now thought to have around 500 million adherents.[6] By contrast the number of active Catholics in England declines, following in the footsteps of the Church of England – which has for many years been seen to dilute traditional Christian doctrines both nationally and locally – always with the best intentions.

I shall return in Chapter 4 to some of the reasons why the demand of tough obedience can itself be attractive to many. But this evidence strongly supports the view that maintaining a distinct identity through tribal badges and demanding doctrines strengthens a community and increases its appeal. And loss of identity has the opposite effect. The evidence also suggests that in the unlikely event of the Church yielding its moral teaching to democratic demand it would soon be on its knees – and praying for the Gates of Hell to keep their proper distance.

I would propose these preliminary conclusions: that the Church must restore, maintain and enhance the distinctness of its identity through its visible signs of unity, holiness, universality, apostolic tradition in its faithfulness to the doctrine of Christ, which brooks no compromise. However, one should not infer a conservative agenda; on the contrary I will argue that it requires radical and perhaps painful change from what it was once and what it is today. Nor should it lead to a ghetto mentality; since Paul withstood Peter in the matter of the Gentiles the Church has seen its mission as the whole world. The more it interacts with the secular, and of course with other religions, the more it needs a distinct identity and a clarity about its contribution. Above all there is one visible sign which predominates because it was specified by Christ: 'By this all will know that you are my disciples, if you love one another.'[7]

Centralization and Autonomy

I referred in my Introduction to the centralizing tendency through which the Church has sought to bring matters under control. But the decline in practice has continued. It could be argued that this is because the situation has gone too far to be recovered. At least this suggests that a further tightening or even, if that were possible, a complete return to the legalistic model would be counterproductive. In fact the ultimate destination of increasing centralization, which may indeed achieve an appearance of unity, is totalitarianism. It is not a climate in which love grows. It inhibits personal commitment to common objectives, it turns responsible and intelligent human beings into moral infants, it continually extends the bounds of declared orthodoxy – and thus brings even the essentials into disrepute. Above all it turns a freely chosen love into obedience. We have to find a better way.

> Derek Wright in his *The Psychology of Moral Behaviour* (Penguin, 1971) notes that members of organized religions are not measurably more altruistic (inclined to love their neighbours) than others. He posits the idea that the majority of religious adherents are concerned with social status and psychological needs to belong. They tend to be less altruistic than the ordinary population. But the minority who are genuinely committed to the ideals of their religion are more altruistic (p. 148). The evidence for the effect of religious affiliation on moral behaviour is sparse and inconclusive. The aspects in which the 'religious' tend to be more conventionally moral tend to be those favoured by the naturally conformist personality. He also suggests that while the apparent purpose of the great religions is to inspire a mature moral autonomy, this tends not to be encouraged by the institutions since it may lower psychological dependence on their authority (pp. 236–7).

There have been notable changes in the attitudes of Western society since World War II. The touched forelock which characterized a stable society in which people knew their place and deferred to those in authority is now history. People have a wide range of possible lifestyles and choices; they see themselves as autonomous and defend strongly what they see as their right to pursue their personal needs. This is accompanied by an ignorance, in both senses of the word, of the past and its values. History does not matter: it is my future which counts and about which I must decide. Experience has ceased to be a continuous growth out of the past but a series of discrete points, symbolized by the digital revolution. Catholics are not immune to this.

To the extent that these attitudes can be held responsible it is hard to see how they can be reversed, although the possibility of a pendulum swing cannot be discounted. The best practical strategy would be to meet this new autonomy head on and help the Church, and ultimately the world, to distinguish between true and false autonomy and to separate the elements of the past which are of no value from those which should still be informing us today. Universality, a distinguishing mark of the Church, requires that it should be able to communicate credibly with the spirit of our times, to test that spirit and 'hold fast what is good'.[8]

A Trigger Event?

However, there is evidence that there is a more immediate factor. Father Greeley reports that the decline in Catholic practice in the USA, which I note above, has not been matched by a similar decline in Protestant congregations, who have been exposed to similar influences. For instance the decline in confidence in Church leaders has been at a substantially higher rate than among Protestants, and the belief in the wrongness of premarital sex is proportionately three times higher among young Protestants. He concludes that the phenomenon of decline is uniquely Catholic and that it is linked to changing attitudes on sex and authority *and to nothing else that we can specify* (Greeley's italics).

Of course practical disagreement with orthodox moral teaching at the personal level is not a new occurrence; St Paul inveighed against it among the earliest Christians.[9] Michael Hornsby-Smith, the English sociologist, tells us that compliance among the laity has 'always been partial and problematic'. The difference is that it is public, openly supported and debated. As long as the articulation of dissent was confined to the bedroom, it caused no crisis. Hornsby-Smith's *Roman*

Catholics Beliefs in England (Cassell, 1991) indicates that most lay Catholics, including those who are highly committed, are deciding 'that these areas (contraception, divorce, abortion) are not the business of the priests, though their guidance may still be acceptable, and that final decision-making must be left to those most concerned to make up their minds'. He reports that it was hard to find a Catholic unambiguously in agreement with the Church's teaching on contraception, and those who were came mostly from the group of practising elderly.[10] No similar general studies of English Catholic belief have been published since then – and perhaps another look is overdue. However, a recent survey established that, although the proportion of Catholics who attended services regularly in 1990 was the same in 2000, the proportion of those claiming to be Catholic but only attending services never or rarely had doubled over the decade. The inference is that there is an increasing tendency for those whose practice is irregular to become more and more nominal in their religious affiliation – and consequently less and less likely to hear, let alone respond to, calls to return.[11]

The steep decline in Catholic practice and response to authority is attributed by these and others to the publication of *Humanae Vitae*; and Hornsby-Smith suggests that the teaching of Vatican II on the autonomy of conscience paved the way. However, the principle of the autonomous conscience goes well beyond sexual and connected morality, and moral theologians and others have developed their ideas over a broad front – and not always in a way acceptable to the Magisterium, as *Veritatis Splendor* indicates.

The Deeper Issue

My bird's-eye review of possible reasons for the gross decline in practice and acceptance of the Church's moral authority suggests that several causes are likely to be involved, though many would argue that the coinciding of the decline and the decision of *Humanae Vitae* predominates. Yet I suspect that this is ultimately an incomplete reading of the situation. The fundamental issue is the exercise of authority and how this relates to the autonomy of the individual within the Church. *Humanae Vitae* brought people up against an immediate practical issue of great personal importance. The tensions which beforehand had affected only a few now affected a broad range of ordinary Catholics. Over the intervening years the ruling of *Humanae Vitae* has ceased for many to be an issue; it just doesn't arise. But it has left behind a much deeper problem: absolute authority is seamless – the failure of a single stitch can lead to the unravelling of the whole fabric. Must the Church grit its teeth and maintain its unquestioned authority, or can it come to look at the use of authority in a very different way – a way which exchanges the use of dictatorial power for the power of influence? This tension has often been encountered in the secular world where the former power of master over man has had perforce to be abandoned, and new ways of leading and managing people have developed. One view might be that the nature of the Church's authority is so different from the secular institution that little if anything is transferable; the other might be that the fundamental principles of authority and its relationship to human nature are universal, and that therefore the Church can learn a great deal from secular experience in this matter. This book will argue the latter view, and attempt to show that what the Church says about herself requires fundamental change in the way in which she exercises her authority. Autonomy and external authority are compatible – although they are permanently in a dynamic balance which precludes the simple formulae of absolute authority on the one hand and unfettered freedom on the other.

Notes to Chapter 1

1. John XXIII, 1961, 1963.
2. *Tablet* (19 June 1999).
3. Andrew Greeley, *Catholics in the 20th Century: A Prelude to the Millennium.* This and other articles on his website at www.agreeley.com.

4. Statistics from various published sources quoted by Garry Wills in *Papal Sin* (Darton, Longman and Todd, 2000).

5. *A New Catholic Commentary on Sacred Scripture* (Nelson, 1969), 105a.

6. www.churchnet.org.uk/news/files3/news374.html, and other sites.

7. John 13.35.

8. 1 Thess. 4.21.

9. Gal. 5.16–26.

10. We should not forget the heroic work done by those who promote and teach natural methods of contraception. They emphasize that many both within and outside the Church come to them for assistance with both contraception and the correction of infertility.

11. Analysis performed for the author by Alison Park, Research Director, National Centre for Social Research.

CHAPTER 2

THE SOVEREIGNTY OF CONSCIENCE

Homo Sapiens is distinguished from the brute beast by two outstanding characteristics: the freedom of will and the use of reason. It follows that it is in the exercise of these characteristics that he may most completely live up to his dignity as a person created in the image of God. His freedom is not random because it is guided by his reason which is ordered towards the good. But in practice his judgement is often so circumscribed by internal and external forces that its scope is limited. And the tension between autonomy and obligation is continuous.

A quick trawl through *Veritatis Splendor* would suggest that autonomy is a dangerous concept; in many passages Pope John Paul is concerned to deal with 'false autonomy' – or the ways in which he claims that modern man, sometimes with the encouragement of moral theologians, mistakes his true freedom within the law of God for the right to make decisions disregarding that law. His preoccupation is understandable given that the major objective of the document is to correct tendencies which he sees as mistaken.

The Pope gives, as a starting point, a picture of what autonomy should mean and why it is important. His description is largely based on the Vatican II document 'The Church in the Modern World' (*Gaudium at Spes*).[1] Here we read that the actual process of employing our freedom to make decisions in line with the good, as we discern it, is willed by God: 'It is he who created man in the beginning, and he left him in the power of his own inclination.'[2] The purpose of this freedom, *Gaudium et Spes* continues, is that through its exercise man is able to 'spontaneously seek his creator and by cleaving to him perfect himself so as to be ready for heaven. Man's dignity then demands that he should act in accordance with a free and conscious choice, personally, inwardly persuaded, and not by either blind impulse from within or coercion from without.' So our freedom is necessary if we are to choose salvation; and by the same token it leaves us free to choose damnation. As Robert Ingersoll, the American freethinker, put it in his *Lectures and Essays*: 'In nature there are neither rewards nor punishments – there are consequences.' Or as the old proverb says: 'Take what you want, says God, then pay for it.' No wonder autonomy makes us nervous.

Autonomy means, through its etymology, law as fashioned by ourselves. But, as I note above, our judgements are not random; a decision made through tossing a coin may enable us to decide but it is not a judgement of reason because that requires some criterion with which to make comparison. That criterion must be the good as we see it; as St Thomas Aquinas puts it: 'every agent acts for an end under the aspect of good'.[3] Of course the view of good may be perverted, as when a criminal sees robbing a bank as good, but, as I discuss below, uncontaminated reason is ordered to recognize the true good through natural law and thus as the will of God for us. This does not contradict autonomy because although this law is objective it can only be recognized through our internal grasp of conscience. It is no loss of my freedom to recognize that I should not steal library books, and to act on that.

Further questions are raised when we encounter a moral teaching of the Church which we are unable to verify through our own reason, and I will return to this in Chapter 5. We might note at this point that a response of obedience to authority, unless we can verify its conformity to the good through our own understanding, is an exercise of diminished autonomy. It operates at, so to speak, second hand by judging that the authority is a more reliable source of the truth than we, in this instance, are able to be.

Autonomy implies responsibility. There is an inclination in our society to place responsibility anywhere but on ourselves. It may lie in our genes, in our upbringing, in the pressures of society. There are a thousand possible reasons with enough possible truth behind them to excuse us. But the autonomous person does not accept such excuses readily. He knows that it is only to the extent that he accepts responsibility for his judgements that he exercises his freedom to be and to grow as a human being. The development of autonomy is a duty for the Christian; correspondingly the Church has an obligation to be a community in which autonomy can thrive and is continually encouraged.

The history of the Church's understanding of the autonomous conscience is as long as the history of the Church itself. The story need not detain us here, although I will need from time to time to refer to certain aspects. Good accounts are available.[4] For our purpose I will confine myself to essential points.

The First Element of Conscience – Recognition of Moral Obligation

Conscientia est omnis divisa in partes tres, as Caesar might have put it had he been a moral theologian. The first of the three elements of conscience in my analysis is the innate recognition, available to all human beings who are not mentally immature or infirm, that we ought to follow good and avoid evil. At first sight this principle appears to have no content; it is as if we have done no more than to define good as that which we ought to follow and evil as that which we ought to avoid. The key is the word 'ought' – our sense that we recognize that we have moral obligations which stem from a different and deeper motivation than ordinary causality. This quality of oughtness has often been attacked by secular critics. For example, Freud maintained that it finds its source in the superego which results from internalizing the commands of our parents while being unaware of their source. Others have claimed that it is no more than a conditioning brought about by general social influences. Some modern philosophers maintain that it has no moral meaning (indeed that there is no such thing as moral meaning) but is merely a matter of taste or instinctive reaction. This (I am serious) is endearingly known as the 'Boo! Hurrah!' approach.

However, the rigour of modern philosophy warns us that the existence of the principle cannot be logically demonstrated. I can do no more than say that while I acknowledge my genetic and educational debt to my parents and am certainly aware of the pressures of society I nevertheless recognize this principle inside myself. I am aware of oughtness as a specific perception quite unlike anything else. And I find it hard to believe that any philosopher contemplating, say, Timothy McVeigh, the Oklahoma Bomber, would justify his crime because it was merely the result of his faulty education or his personal preference.

The Second Element of Conscience – Distinguishing Good and Evil

How do we recognize good and evil? This brings us to the second element of conscience. We do so by applying our reason to our fundamental nature and deducing from that what is in accordance with it and what is contrary to it. This is the basis of the natural law. We associate this concept particularly with Thomas Aquinas but he was baptizing Aristotle's thinking by attributing its source to God.[5] A remarkably clear statement comes from the first century BC:

> There is indeed a true law – right reason – that is in harmony with Nature and present in all things, unchanging and eternal and that guides us to our duty by its commands and deflects us from wrongdoing by its prohibitions. Its commands and prohibitions never fail to prevail with the good but they have no power to influence the wicked. It is not right to legislate against the requirements of this law and it is not permitted to limit its application. It is impossible for it to be repealed in its entirety and we cannot be exempted from this law even by the Roman people or by the Senate. We do not need to seek out a Sextus Aelius to interpret or expound this law nor will there be one law in Rome, another in Athens, one law at one time and a different one some time later. One eternal and unchanging law will govern all peoples at all times and it will be, as it were, the single ruling and commanding god of the whole human race. That god is the creator of the law, its proclaimer and its enforcer. The man who does not obey this law is denying his own nature and, by rejecting his human nature, he will incur the greatest of punishments, even though he will have evaded the other things that are thought of as penalties. (Cicero, *De Republica* III. xxii)

The earliest secular reference of which I am aware comes from Sophocles' *Antigone* (442 BC) where Antigone says to the king: 'I did not think your commands had the power to overcome the unwritten and unchangeable laws of God and heaven, for you are only a man.' The first Christian reference comes from St Paul: '[The Gentiles] show that what the law requires is written on their hearts, while their conscience also bears witness and their conflicting thoughts accuse or perhaps excuse them.'[6] For this and for its fundamental rationality, it has become and remains the principal way in which the Church has seen right and wrong. It is not a law of nature like the law of gravity, but a moral demand which arises from the nature of human beings. For example we recognize that since man is a social animal his nature requires that he should keep his promises – without which society is impossible.

Some important conclusions emerge from this. The first is that the demand of the natural law comes from God who created human nature. The second is that it exists independently of us. Although we may only detect it from looking within ourselves we are trying to discern a truth which lies outside ourselves. Pope John Paul in *Veritatis Splendor* emphasizes this distinction.[7] The third is that the natural law is accessible to all, Christians or not. Everyone is bound. Accordingly moral judgements have a universal quality. Its demands applied to the first true human being as to the Middle Ages as to today. And when I say, for instance, that lying is wrong I mean that it is as wrong for the Polynesian as for the Native American as for the gent in his London club; we all share human nature.

> Although natural law is not the same as a law of nature there is an illuminating analogy that can be drawn. I cannot break a law of nature – if, for instance, I attempt to break the law of gravity by jumping over a cliff I only end up by breaking myself. If I break the natural law, even inadvertently, I end up by doing harm to myself and others.[8]

Many moral philosophers have difficulties with the concept of natural law[9] and they usually continue by suggesting their own basis for morality. However, these alternatives are quickly opposed by their colleagues who, in turn, suggest their own. But natural law has one irrefutable advantage: when in the ordinary way people dispute moral questions they make natural law assumptions. You and I cannot usefully argue about what constitutes a lie unless we have a common starting point in the value of truth; we cannot dispute about abortion unless we share a concept of the special quality of human life. We may disagree about how it applies in the question at issue but that is another matter. Similarly moral philosophers often find themselves appealing to natural law judgements when criticizing the work of others or defending their own. This confirms that natural law, perhaps by another name, is profoundly in accord with human reason and, as St Paul says, written into our hearts.

However, there is a problem. 'Written' in this context is a metaphor and there is room for plenty of argument. The difficulty does not lie with the top level of general principles – for example, that we ought not to do harm to others. But as we get into the extension of the principle things become more uncertain. What does doing harm constitute? Would it allow me to pursue my own lawful interests even if others are harmed thereby? Can I sentence another to prison? And who are others? If they are persons do the mentally defective come into that category, or an embryo at an early stage of development? Should animals be included, and, if so, how about fleas? Aristotle taught in his *Politics*[10] that slavery was acceptable because slaves were naturally constituted for the task and regarded as chattels or even as a kind of extension of their master. Just as you do no wrong by harming your own possessions, he argues, so you can do no wrong by harming your slave. Aquinas tells us that as we get further down into detail there is increasing room for disagreement.[11] Even recording the principles in stone, as in the Ten Commandments, is no more than a starting point.

Aquinas continues by looking at more reasons why we might fail in our grasp of natural law. We may be led astray through the false values of our own society. He cites the Germans who, according to Julius Caesar, do not consider stealing wrong. Our own society has moved in fifty years from a general abhorrence for abortion to a general, if uneasy, acceptance and, following from that, to the cloning of embryos to breed useful tissues. We see how a new development is initially greeted by general concern, but soon becomes the respectable norm – only to create a precedent for the next stage. And the long established status quo, example, education and habit may well blunt our awareness of the good. The influence of Aristotle and the convenience of the slave system are the likely reasons for the Church failing to condemn slavery for hundreds of years. The Australian settlers in the early nineteenth century shot Aborigines as if they were kangaroos and no doubt thought they were doing a social service. In the sad history of the twentieth century we have seen how men can escape from the internal demand of the natural law by convincing themselves that those they wish to dispose of are somehow a sub-species, not really human at all.[12] Our bad dispositions and bad choices increasingly blind us to the natural law. To summarize Pope John Paul, seeking and following the good makes us more aware and more accurate in our perception. The opposite leads us towards increasing error.[13]

I should note here a deduction from natural law which has its own particular set of problems. There has been a prevalent view in moral theology that we can discover the natural law in two ways: one is through applying our reason to man's nature and realizing, for instance, that, being a social animal, there is an obligation to keep promises; and the second is by reading God's intentions from the physical structures and functions of the body. Traditionally the first category, stemming from human reason, is governed in its application by the discrimination of human reason; the second, being directly ordained by God, gives rise to moral prohibitions which always apply, irrespective of circumstances. By and large this applies to sexual matters – for instance the classical cases of contraceptive or homosexual acts. I want to look at this in more detail in an example in an Appendix because there are strong arguments for questioning whether this uncompromising approach to natural law, despite its long history, is valid.

The Third Element of Conscience – Judging Our Actions

So much for the general background to conscience. The third element is the practical application of these principles to the judgement we have to make, or to judge an action we have taken. In the simplest terms we need to judge whether or not the decision is in accordance with the good. But it can be a very complex matter. What happens if a gang of terrorists calls at my house with the intention of kneecapping my friend, who is hiding upstairs? When they ask me if he is in my home do I say yes, or no, or refuse to answer? Since I have adapted this example from Cardinal Newman, one of whose greatest works was triggered by this dilemma,[14] I will not develop it here. But I do return to it briefly in considering the way natural law has been applied to lying (Appendix).

The process of judgement is known as the formation of conscience. In practice it may be long or short, simple or complex. But reason tells us that we have an obligation to form it in a way which is adequate to the matter in hand, taking into account the time available if it is urgent. The objective is to discern the truth – that is the good which is found in the correspondence of the action with human nature as God created it. It follows that to fail to seek the truth makes our justification empty of worth. I devote Chapters 5 and 6 to the main issues involved in forming conscience.

The Sovereignty of Conscience

It is a truism in both reason and theology that conscience is sovereign. That is, we are bound to follow the judgement of our conscience even if it be in error. If a cannibal judges that capturing and eating enemies is a good demanded of him then he is bound to follow that judgement, although the action itself remains evil and damaging. We may of course, as a result of *our* judgement of conscience, be bound to stop him. If that seems an extreme example Aquinas is, for his own time, equally extreme when he says that if a man's judgement instructs him to reject belief in Christ then he must do so. Conversely someone who intends to do evil but through his error actually does good commits an evil through the misdirection of his will.[15]

In Robert Bolt's *Man for all Seasons*,[16] the character of Thomas More explicitly grounds his conscience (in the matter of the Apostolic Succession) not on the truth or otherwise but on the belief he personally has. The focus is on the rights of his independent *ego*, not on the discovery of objective truth. In fact More claimed his conclusion was based on seven years' study of the question. Bolt's More was claiming that his right of conscience was based on his decision; that is, entirely subjective. The real More knew that it had to be based on his best endeavour to discover the objective truth. This antithesis shows clearly the difference between the common modern approach to conscience and the traditional approach.

Vatican II's document *The Church in the Modern World* speaks succinctly on the sovereignty of conscience, whether it be true or mistaken. It includes this passage: 'Conscience is the most secret core and sanctuary of a man. There he is alone with God whose voice echoes in his depths.'[17] This conception of an immediate encounter with God – no intermediaries – is fundamental to our understanding. The encounter – though it may not always be recognized as such – is in the light of our common human nature as present for unbelievers as it is for believers.

Imagine man, naked to the world, making his first decisions about how he should discover the good he ought to follow and the evil he ought to avoid. This stage is logically prior to any acceptance that God exists; and he may, as many do, proceed to develop moral norms through the application of his reason. Or he may recognize through his judgement the existence of the creative power of God. As the source of all reality, God's law and the moral demands of reality are the same. At some later point he will have to judge whether Christ is truly the revelation of God amongst us. Then he must judge whether the Church is the community founded by Christ to which he must adhere. He must then make a judgement about the authority of the Church to witness to God's law, and the various levels of that authority.

Forgive the naivety of this thought-experiment. It introduces an important point. I, as a cradle Catholic, enter this process at the latest stage: that of the Church's authority. I take the earlier stages for granted. But conscience judges backwards as well as forwards. At God's own Judgement Day I will have to answer even for my judgement that God exists. It will be a good defence that I looked for him as best I could but did not find him, and became an agnostic or an atheist. It will not be a good defence to say I never really looked into the matter – any more than the Australian settler who ignored the prompting about the duty he owed to the Aborigines. It may come as a shock to see Bertrand Russell ushered through the pearly gates while Sister X who knows her Catechism by heart has to wait in the queue. But it could be. Similarly the other judgements in the thought-experiment remain my personal responsibility.

A much argued question is whether an individual sincerely following what happens to be an objectively erroneous conscience is performing a meritorious act. That is, although he would sin in not following his conscience, it does not automatically follow that he does good in so doing. But the old tag 'an act is good if every aspect is good, and bad if any aspect is evil'[18] does not seem to do justice to the separation between subjective intention and objective truth. I would argue that all acts performed with good intentions and responsibly formed conscience are meritorious, and in doing so would be in line with a strong tradition of moral theology led by Alphonsus Liguori. However, *Veritatis Splendor* (para. 63) tells us that choosing an act which is in fact evil does not prevent the bad effects of the evil nor does it contribute to our closer understanding of what the good requires.[19]

That is a brief account and I realize that it requires nuanced development, particularly in the matter of the extent of the Church's moral authority. (It will receive this in Chapter 5.) But it is the only way which expresses for me the fundamental sovereignty of conscience which goes to the centre of what man is.

A Note on Fundamentalism

Fundamentalism has spread from its original dictionary definition as adherence to a literal interpretation and acceptance of Scripture to cover a broader range. So we can talk of the fundamentalism which justified the slaughter of tens of thousands of Christians by other Christians of a different persuasion. Similarly we can talk of Islamic fundamentalists whose understanding of the Koran, the Prophet and the will of Allah leads them to conclusions which are repudiated by many of their fellow adherents, and are unacceptable to Christians. When I left school after ten years of Catholic education I maintained the smug fundamentalist certainty that I knew the ultimate truths, and that those who denied them would be condemned for their intransigence. (I speak of several decades ago.)

The common factor in fundamentalism appears to be the acceptance of an authority which is not open to question, and which rules every other consideration. It is the antithesis of autonomy, which is the deadly enemy of fundamentalism. It is only when we take personal responsibility for our choices, including the choice of accepting an external authority, that we counter fundamentalism. Only in making reason our ultimate instrument of judgement can we maintain our dignity as human beings. Exchanging reason for blind obedience is to wound our humanity, made in the image of God. Those who promote blind obedience are the blind leading the blind. And we all know where they end up.

Notes to Chapter 2

1. *Veritatis Splendor* 38 ff; *Gaudium et Spes* 17.
2. Sirach 15.14.
3. *Summa Theologica* I II 94.2.
4. Linda Hogan in her *Confronting the Truth* (Darton, Longman and Todd, 2001) brings us up to date; Eric D'Arcy's *Conscience and Its Right to Freedom* (Sheed and Ward, 1961) is more detailed and particularly strong on Aquinas.

5. *Nicomachean Ethics* (*passim*); see also Plato's *Republic*.
6. Rom. 2.15.
7. See, for instance 32 and 55 (last paragraph).
8. I owe this analogy to Frank Sheed. I cannot give a further reference because my copy of his *Theology and Sanity* (Sheed and Ward) was borrowed many years ago by a low church minister who was prominent in the media at the time. He was evidently so impressed, as indeed he might be, that I am still waiting for him to return it.
9. A fundamental objection, first expressed in Plato's *Euthyphro*, states that if God is the author of the natural law then we are merely obeying his arbitrary command; if he is not, why bring God into it at all? This objection depends on an anthropomorphic view of God as some sort of super-elevated human being. But the Judaeo-Christian concept of God is that in him the essence of reality and his will are one. He who Is. So the objection disappears.
10. Book 1, 4–5.
11. *Summa Theologica* I II 94.4.
12. It has been said that mortal sin is impossible for the English since they are constitutionally unable to focus their minds sufficiently for the purpose.
13. *Veritatis Splendor* 64.
14. *Apologia Pro Vita Sua.*
15. *Summa Theologica* I II 9.5.
16. Samuel French, 1960.
17. *Gaudium et Spes* 16.
18. *Bonum ex integra causa, malum ex quocumque defectu.*
19. Charles Curran discusses this in *The Catholic Moral Tradition Today* (Georgetown University Press, 1999), p. 88 and footnote.

CHAPTER 3

THE INTEGRATION OF LOVE AND LAW

In the previous chapter about conscience you may have noticed that the word 'love' did not occur. Nor does it occur, except in a collo-quial sense, in Cardinal Newman's brilliant essay on conscience in his *Letter to the Duke of Norfolk*,[1] to which I will return. Conscience is a process of choosing good and avoiding evil and it has equal appli-cation to all. But the central message of Christ is that loving God and loving your neighbour are not only the greatest commandments, but on them depend the whole law and the prophets.[2] In the New Testament dispensation we learn that it is Christ who saves and not the law, and that we open ourselves to his salvation through our faith and love.

'Love and do what you will', said St Augustine.[3] Some have taken this as an invitation to licence.[4] But St Paul, after citing the social commandments, says that these 'and any other commandment, are summed up in the sentence, "You shall love your neighbour as yourself." Love does no wrong to a neighbour; therefore love is the fulfilling of the law.'[5] This integration of love and law makes sense. In pursuing the good through our understanding and application of the natural law we seek the good of ourselves and our neighbours; the Commandments list the principles which mark the lower limits of love. Cross the line and love is denied; above the line there is, literally, infinite room to soar. Thus law is no longer an imposition from outside; the Commandments merely articulate what we realize deeply inside ourselves. Our Christian freedom is not under the law but within the law written in our hearts.

31

The Emphasis on Law

So Catholic teaching must and does give prominence to the law of the Commandments and to what gives them meaning as a way to salvation – the law of love. Not surprisingly a different degree of practical emphasis is given at different historical times. In the early Middle Ages such systematic moral teaching as there was then was primarily concerned with the Sacrament of Reconciliation, starting with the listing of appropriate penances and gradually developing over the centuries into systematic manuals of moral theology but retaining a primary focus on matters of sin and law. The atmosphere is well captured by this quote from Father Henry Davis SJ; his four-volume work on moral theology (Sheed and Ward) was a standard. This is taken from the 1958 *Moral and Pastoral Theology* edition.

> The Catholic Church insists therefore, in season and out of season, on the religious education of the child, explicit, dogmatic, determinate moral education in a religious atmosphere, thus giving him something to cling to against the time of vehement temptation. It indoctrinates its children during many years, until resistance to evil becomes an almost second nature. It does not wait until the passions have grown strong then to offer the youth the free choice of religious dogmas or moral antidotes. It says to the child: you must be good in the way I teach you to be good, so that afterwards you may know how to be good.

Although this passage may look archaic to us today it would be unfair to blame Father Davis; he was a child of his times, and we may well wonder how grotesque some of our current attitudes will look a generation or two from now. An interesting comment from the 1960s came from Sister Laurence SND who was reviewing a survey of the attitudes of 600 adolescent girls towards the Sacrament of Reconciliation. Among her comments were: 'It is sobering to reflect that the notion of the autonomy of the human conscience, fundamental to Christianity, has practically disappeared from our teaching.'[6] In another contemporary work John Ford and Gerald Kelly described the moral theologian as 'a sort of criminal lawyer engaged by the defence: "consult so and so. He will get you out of it if anyone can".'[7]

David Lodge's best-selling novel *How Far Can You Go*[8] is set in the early 1950s and deals hilariously with the quandary of young Catholics attempting to match their sexual lives to the Church's teaching. The humour was apposite, but the reality was far from funny – *experto crede*.

Autonomy of conscience might have 'practically disappeared from our teaching' but it was still clearly there. Yet the emphasis and the focus was on law and on obedience to the law. As Father Bernhard Häring put it: 'One who is exclusively concerned with the normative formula without being taken up with the value which is its foundation will inevitably descend to a moribund legality.'[9]

Some Problems in the Emphasis on Law

The problem does not lie with the essential nature of law which acts as a witness to what God asks of us. Otherwise we would be asking Moses to take the tablets of stone back up the mountain and return them to their inscriber. The problem lies with the legalistic cast of mind. It emerges in three major ways.

The first is that the laws, or the inferences from the laws, simply multiply. Regulation breeds regulation which, in turn, breeds regulation. Necessary exceptions and qualifications breed further regulations until the whole horizon of human possibilities is filled with regulation. This is not necessarily all bad. General Catholic moral teaching is wise, profound and invaluable, as I shall emphasize in Chapter 6. But the legalistic mentality tends to cover the whole system with a blanket authority. If missing Mass one Sunday, allowing oneself a few moments of lecherous thought, or putting granny through the mincer are all mortal sins then discrimination between them seems pointless – the switch between heaven and hell is either on or off. Questions of love can disappear if the key to the moral life depends on a book of rules.

This then leads to casuistry. Casuistry is simply the application of the rules to particular cases and, in principle and often in practice, is a most valuable and merciful service. I give some examples in Chapter 5. But it has a bad name; we associate it with finding loopholes. Pascal in his seventeenth-century *Lettres Provinciales*, which was directed against the Jesuit casuists, quotes authorities who teach that, although duelling is lawful since it is self-defence against an attack on one's fortune or one's honour, it is better to kill one's enemy by stealth since you avoid unnecessarily risking your life and you save yourself from co-operating in the sin which your enemy commits by duelling.[10] Admittedly this is an extreme example of how far casuistry can go, and Pascal was making a case, but it does indicate where the legalistic attitude can lead. Father Davis (see above) provides us with a more recent and, in its time, more understandable example:

> It is not, as a general rule, permitted to Catholic nurses in hospitals to send for non-Catholic ministers to attend non-Catholic patients for religious purposes; they must be passive in such cases (Sacred Office March 15 1858). This was further explained (Feb 5 1872) to mean that nurses might tell some non-Catholic attendant that the patient wanted the non-Catholic minister, and this was declared not to be active co-operation. Furthermore, if even this were found impossible, then for very grave reasons and to prevent enmity arising against the Church, nurses might themselves send for the non-Catholic minister if asked to do so.

Fortunately, he tells us that it would be in order for the Catholic nurse to prepare a table with flowers, since this is not a religious act, but she must not of course join in the prayers. Nor, incidentally, should she ever wear internal sanitary protection since this is forbidden for both physical and moral reasons. Davis records this ruling in the decent obscurity of a learned language. However, I have read elsewhere that she would be excused this last prohibition if she happened to be a ballet dancer.

The second problem lies in its tendency towards seeing obedience to the law as the objective of the moral life. Obedience is a virtue in many circumstances, but in the matter of conscience it only applies in a very specific sense. Our obedience here is only directed at the truth. We are obedient to God by responding to the laws of reality to be discovered in the nature of his creation. No intermediary can save us from that responsibility. This is in no way to attack the authority of the Church in expounding these laws of reality and their applications, but they can only bind in so far as we see them as corresponding to the truth. Of course this simple statement needs amplification, which it will get in Chapter 5.

In providing a comprehensive network of law and its applications there is an inherent tendency to discourage moral autonomy. Attempting to discern the truth and developing an ever greater sensitivity towards it is fundamental to Christian growth. We aim to become, one might say, a moral person down to our very roots. But if the pre-packed answers are already to hand it is likely that this important process will be inhibited. Why should I go to all the trouble of trying to find the moral good in a situation if I can simply look the answer up? And so the power and habit of conscience become atrophied through disuse.

> When Irish girls came to England to have abortions, the practice being illegal in their country, they were asked why they had not used contraceptives. To which they pointed out that their priests had told them that contraception was wrong. It apparently had not occurred to them that abortion might be more wrong. In fact they could have quoted the authority of Aquinas for holding that artificial contraception was worse than fornication.[11]

The third problem is that it leads to minimalism. That is, it conveys the idea that the Christian vocation is fulfilled by keeping inside the law. A minimalist avoids stealing, a Christian is asked to respect and preserve another's property. The minimalist avoids telling a lie, a Christian is called to convey the whole of the truth his neighbour needs. The minimalist does not commit adultery, a Christian is called to respect his chastity and that of others to the fullest extent. The Beatitudes and the Sermon on the Mount indicate the Christian call – they are the law as transformed by the superior law of love. And always that challenge: 'You, therefore, must be perfect, as your heavenly father is perfect.'[12]

The Emphasis on Love

The modern movement away from legalism to love in moral theology seems to have been first recorded in 1922 when Father Arthur Vermeersch's *Theologiae Moralis Principia, Responsa, Consilia* (Gregorian University Press) appeared, but the most comprehensive account (known to me) is Father Häring's *Lex Christi*.[13] The emphasis is not directly on obedience to law or even on self-perfection. It is on entering more and more into dialogue with the living Christ and Christ-in-neighbour. It is in fact a constant movement towards the ultimate integration with Christ that characterizes the resurrection of the body. Every aspect of the Christian life is seen in these terms and judged by them, but in specific cases the law sets out the limits of the relationship. It is a response of person to person, not a reaction of person to law. The impact of this can be tremendous, transforming the sterility of the letter into something personal, rich, developing. No longer am I concerned with conformity, seeing a kind of perfection in my adherence to the law; on the contrary the goal is Christ and my full relationship with him. He is the harbour light and the laws are the buoys which mark the entrance to the channel. 'The ten commandments protect the outer periphery of the realm in which Christ will be formed in us.'[14]

Some Problems with the Emphasis on Love

I need scarcely point out that achieving the goal of love and allowing Christ to be formed within us is hard, and of course a work of Grace. Few of us can contemplate that call without a sense of shame at how little we have responded to it. But here I want to look at some more mundane issues.

We use the word 'love' in different senses. Sometimes we mean love as a general attitude oriented towards the good of another or indeed ourselves – *agape* as the Greeks called it. It is always related, at least implicitly, to God and constitutes a major way in which he made us in his image. Sometimes we mean desire – ordinary desire or sexual desire. Desire is a natural and necessary gift of God and should be valued according to its nature. But it is a feeling which is essentially oriented to what *we* want. In our lives both elements are intermixed, and desire potentially provides a strong support for love, or may call us towards love in the first place. But the mixture is subtle and we often confuse the two, as St John of the Cross warns us in his *Dark Night of the Soul.*

An important contribution made by the legalistic approach is to avoid this confusion by leaving the word 'love' out of it altogether. The emphasis on love is all too easily transmuted into a wishy-washy soft-edged concept into which anything may be fitted. The question 'what does love demand?' can so easily become 'what do I want?' or 'what do I desire?' Many critics of the love approach to morals claim, and adduce strong evidence in support, that, within both the world and the Church, a choice of action is often justified by love without making a distinction between love and desire. *What I want* drags reason in its train and so easily becomes the criterion by which we judge what is right and what is wrong. Thus the concept of an objective moral law gives place to a subjective moral law whose only reference point is within ourselves.

Of course this need not be. The root of the misunderstanding may lie in the fact that the word 'love' is used in mid-air, as if it had an independent existence of its own. Yet even absolute love in the divine nature exists in relationship, and there is no human experience of love that does not, whether it is man to God, man to man, parent to child or spouse to spouse. Each relationship makes certain concrete demands that derive from the nature of the persons within the relationship and the principle of the relationship itself. So we are back to the moral law again – defining the lower boundary to our love and calling us upwards to a more complete fulfilment.

But the problem does not go away. We have failed in communi-cating this essential integration between love and law. And what we are so often left with is love at the expense of law, or law at the expense of love. At least, apparently. We would expect to find that looking at moral questions primarily through love will give in some cases a different answer from looking primarily through law. It could throw up instances where we find the law is inappropriate (remember that the more detailed the application of natural law the more uncertain it becomes), or needs to be nuanced, or may take a different level of priority. This does not mean that law is not a witness to the imperatives of love; on the contrary, just as the law points in the direction of love so it is informed and refined by love in its turn. A simple example of this is provided by the starving man who steals bread in order to survive. The law says that stealing is forbidden, but the plain man – informed by love – cannot accept this. So the Church reviews her understanding of the law and concludes that the right of every man to receive sustenance takes priority over the law against stealing. A similar example occurs in the case of kidney donation which on a *prima facie* basis involves self-mutilation. I discuss this in the Appendix. This distinction clarifies the role of autonomy in the moral life. Moral choice based on blind obedience is, as I have already noted, inconsistent with autonomy. Moral choice based on love presupposes autonomy, but reason requires that we take the proper steps to discern what love demands.

A result of confusing what we ought to do with what we want to do leads Pope John Paul to regret the loss of our sense of sin. He quotes Pius XII to the effect that the sin of the twentieth century is the loss of the sense of sin.[15] It follows of course that if the decisions of conscience are validated merely by subjective prejudice and without concern for the truth sin cannot find an interstice in which to fit. Perhaps a difficulty here is that the word 'sin' is a label which carries so many old-fashioned connotations that we do not easily relate to it. The Hebrew and Greek words for sin in the Bible mean 'missing the mark'; I find that a valuable insight. If our sense of sin is rephrased as an acceptance that we have chosen to miss the mark and thus have done wrong then the situation, at least to me, looks rather different. I may be inaccurate in some of my judgements about how I have done wrong, but I have no doubt that I make that judgement. Similarly I find that most ordinary people, religious or not, have a similar sense. Indeed it could be argued that one of the great inhibitors of moral growth is the false sense of guilt which abounds. Of course the advanced capacity for self-justification which is a feature of public and private life in our time reduces or misdirects our acceptance that we have done wrong; but it is far from a black-and-white picture. I would contend that clear and effective teaching on conscience formation would do much to restore a sense of sin by leading people through an intelligent assessment of moral choices to recognize the mark, and correspondingly a realization of where they have missed it. The teaching Church has its responsibilities in this matter, too.

It is often argued that the legalistic approach has the advantage of certainty. Attempting to direct one's moral choices according to what one sees as the demands of love creates ambiguity and confusion. It has been noted that those with a personality which inclines towards the authoritarian find such ambiguity difficult to live with; they would rather have clear-cut boundaries.[16] But, prescinding from the question of actions which are invariably wrong in themselves (which needs further discussion), life and decisions *are* ambiguous. With increasing experience and wisdom the certainties of our youth evanesce and what once seemed plain and simple turns out to be neither simple nor plain. We have to do our best to thread our way through conflicting options, ready now to yield and now to insist. We try to do our best from decision to decision with the humility to accept that it may not be *the* best. We are stumbling pilgrims and must be thankful that we belong in a stumbling pilgrim Church, content to accept that in the end all manner of things will be well.

Summary

In this chapter I have discussed how love and law are not at variance with each other, but truly integrated. Our relationship to Christ through love is the fundamental vocation, and the law is the guide that God has given us, through both Revelation and reason, to mark the boundary that separates the realm of love from the realm of unlove. We must never let the law predominate because it is a means rather than an end; it can condemn us but it cannot save us. Yet we must never forget that the law bears witness to the truths that are the underpinning of love. It has often been said that there can be no conflict between Revelation, rightly understood, and science, rightly understood, since they are both concerned with the one truth. Similarly, and for the same reason, there can be no conflict between love and law – when they are both rightly understood.

Notes to Chapter 3

1. London: Montague Pickering, 1876.
2. Matt. 5.43. The implication is that it has always been so; the first reference to loving your neighbour occurs in Lev. 19.18. In Rom. 4 St Paul emphasizes that Abraham was justified not by law but by faith, and extends this to all the Jews, as well as Christians. The law has many meanings in the Old Testament, from the comprehensive network of Judaic law and regulations to the basic social commandments. It is to the latter that the New Testament refers.
3. '*Dilige et quod vis fac.*' In *Epist. Joann. Tractatus*, vii, 8.
4. For instance the Satanist Aleister Crowley, who used it as the motto for his debauched group practices.
5. Rom. 13.8–10.
6. *Clergy Review* (February 1966).
7. John C. Ford and Gerald Kelly, *Contemporary Moral Theology*, vol. 1 (Newman Press, 1963).
8. Martin, Secker and Warburg, 1980.
9. *The Law of Christ*, vol. 1 (Newman Press, 1954).
10. *Lettres Provinciales* vii (1656).
11. See *Summa Theologica* II II 154. 12.
12. Matt. 5.43.
13. *Op. Cit.* (n. 9 above).
14. G. Ermecke, *Theologische Quartalscrift*, 131 (1951), 411.
15. Pope Pius XII, Radio Message to the U.S. National Catechetical Congress in Boston (26 October 1946).
16. J. Zacker, 'Authoritarian Avoidance of Ambiguity', *Psychological Reports*, 33 (1973), pp. 901–2.

CHAPTER 4

BECOMING WHAT WE OUGHT TO BE

A long and unsettled dispute in moral philosophy debates whether it is more meritorious to be the sort of person who has to fight very hard to avoid doing evil or to be so naturally oriented towards the good that avoiding evil is an easy task. Fortunately I do not have to settle this question here. We know two things: first, that at some level there is always a struggle. St Paul witnessed to this when he spoke about the constant war between our conflicting tendencies: 'For I do not do the good I want but the evil I do not want is what I do.'[1] The second is that we have a duty to try continuously to become 'good' people. Christianity sees this essentially in our task to become more and more like Christ. But the ancient philosophers also see this clearly as a matter of reason.

It is inevitable that we focus most of the time on right and wrong acts because this has an immediate practical effect on what we do in the here and now. But unfortunately it takes the emphasis away from the importance of our personal formation – becoming the sort of person we ought to be. The two are, of course, interlinked. But they are not the same. The linking is circular: that is, our goodness leads to our taking the right decisions which love demands; and taking those right decisions enhances our moral perceptions and consolidates our orientation towards the good.[2] The circle can, of course, turn both ways. For example an individual who deceives his friend is not only likely to become more and more slack in his attitude towards telling the truth but he will also find it harder, as the habit grows, to recognize what the truth demands. He reinforces his bad tendency.[3]

The Catholic moral system has always included an important emphasis on the development of the virtues. Plato and Aristotle originally categorized the virtues, seeing them as the qualities needed in order to achieve the good life. Aquinas's account gives over-arching significance by extending them to the specifically Christian virtues of Faith, Hope and Charity. The Christian, or 'Theological', virtues are a work of Grace infused in us by God. The secular virtues are accessible through human nature, and lead towards the good, and thus towards God. Not surprisingly they seem to have a slightly musty air about them, attributable to their long history. This does not make them irrelevant since human nature has not changed; but the terminology lacks appeal. So we get a listing of the cardinal virtues as: Prudence, Justice, Fortitude and Temperance. They are called cardinal because they are the 'hinges' on which the multiplicity of other possible virtues turn. But Prudence has a specific meaning – that of practical wisdom in our choices or, as St Augustine put it , 'the knowledge of what to seek and what to avoid'. It does not carry the common overtone of prudence in the sense of being cautious. It comes first in the list, not because it is the most important, but because it governs and directs the other virtues. Justice carries the feel of the courtroom; it is too large a word for our petty experiences. Fortitude is not a word in ordinary usage and does not readily suggest the determination to stick with the right thing despite opposition from within and without – in both large and small matters. And Temperance sounds like avoiding hangovers; it has largely lost its original sense of finding the judicious mean between two possible extremes: courage, for instance, is the mean between foolhardiness and timidity. These old-fashioned terms, while under-standable in their true context, do not readily convey their intended meaning. Perhaps we need some new names. I propose, merely as a trial shot, Practical Wisdom, Fairness, Determination and Balance. And I have no difficulty with the generic name of Hinge Virtues. Others will perhaps have better ideas. Of course, even under new names, each virtue needs explanation and extension, but it is important that they set us off at least in the right direction, and are qualities which are recognizable to all as desirable.

However, it is not the purpose of this chapter to examine these virtues in their formal categories by whatever name. This, together with Faith, Hope and Charity, has been done elsewhere with great thoroughness.[4] Here I want to propose some particular virtues which I believe we would do well to cultivate in our quest to become moral persons. No doubt some or all of these could find a place as extensions of the traditional categories, but I will leave that to others.

First we must go back to St Thomas. He described such virtues as 'habits by which we live righteously'.[5] They are not just dispositions or tendencies because to be virtues the tendency must convert into the corresponding behaviour. 'Virtue is that which makes its possessor good, and his work good likewise.'

The development of the virtues is more central to leading the moral life than moral action. We are called first to love and then to express that love in loving behaviour. Objectively good behaviour is worthless without love, as St Paul make clear in his classic passage: 'If I give away all that I have, and if I deliver my body to be burned, but have not love, I gain nothing.'[6] The focus of morality is not the question 'What should I do?' but 'Who should I become?' And then to set about cultivating the virtues or habits which correspond. The result is not only moral behaviour proceeding, so to speak, from our habitual interior orientation but an increasing sensitivity of moral perception. A person who is growing in goodness will be increasingly open to the law written in his heart, will see it more clearly, and be more motivated to fulfil it. It will not necessarily save him from making moral judgements but he will be conformed by his nature to recognizing what love demands and responding to it.

Where we stand at any one moment in our possession of a virtue depends on a number of variables. Genetic inheritance, upbringing, various experiences in life can all play a part. Just like ordinary habits we have attitudes and responses which come to us from outside; the challenge is to develop the good habits and to discourage the bad ones. It can help to understand the sort of person we are and why our habits are as they are; from this it becomes possible to develop strategies which help us to advance. We can sometimes make a judgement of another's standing in a particular virtue but we cannot know the degree of responsibility since we do not know the starting point. We may, and must try to, make judgements about ourselves

– though often we can do little more than measure progress and regress. As always, the instrument of measurement will be how our decisions and actions change, and what concrete good things result from them.

Inevitably, therefore, the balance of this chapter is not concerned with examining principles and approaches. I will be attempting merely to propose virtues for consideration, accompanied with enough practical detail as is needed to make my proposals clear.

The Virtue of Self-Esteem

To love one's neighbour as oneself implies that we have an obligation to love ourselves. This does not, of course, mean a selfish love. The 'me, me, me' mentality, continually concerned with getting our share, asserting our rights, deifying our own decisions, appears to be a feature of modern society. It can be very destructive, and its error can be seen precisely in the fact that it militates against our love of neighbour instead of leading to it. In Christian terms self-esteem starts with the acceptance that we are lovable; we know this because God loves us, and thought we were worthwhile redeeming. 'But God shows his love for us in that while we were yet sinners Christ died for us.'[7] Secondly, the Church has always taught (contrary to some strains of Protestantism) that through Grace we are made radically holy. Christ's redemptive power is not a sort of whitewash covering a sinful reality – which persists, but changes in our very depths the kind of person we are. There is every reason to value ourselves and be proud of being the children of God.

However, self-esteem is not always easy to achieve. Usually as a result of a combination of previous circumstances some people have a deeply laid habit of devaluing themselves. And all of us – perhaps as a result of some failure – are likely to have periods of this from time to time. We realize that this response is neither rational nor helpful, yet it comes to us very readily.

One effect is false guilt. True guilt comes from realizing that we have done wrong or failed to live up to our aspirations; we repent,

seek forgiveness of God and our neighbour and make what restitution we can. We are left without guilt overhang – just the
resolution to do better. False guilt comes when, knowing that God
has forgiven us, we cannot forgive ourselves; or when we know that
we were not responsible for some regretted outcome but still feel
guilty about it. It is often said that false guilt has been induced in
Catholics by the emphasis in childhood on the multitudinous sins
we were apparently committing. Father Davis's regime for the moral
education of children, quoted in the previous chapter, gives some
support for this. It may or may not not be so, but I have noticed that
many people who had no such upbringing will also have their full
ration of false guilt. Arguably they have more reason since they may
not be aware of the forgiveness of God, or the sacramental channels
to which they can apply. It may even be that Catholics use their
upbringing as an excuse: 'I have no responsibility for my false guilt
since it was induced in me by others.' But whether we had original
responsibility for it or not, we are today responsible for what we do
about it. The human condition is prone to false guilt.

> Derek Wright [see Chapter 1, p. 14] makes the point that false guilt
> can be induced by the parent relating moral values to parental
> approval, as opposed to encouraging the child to understand the
> reasons why. In the first situation guilt or release from guilt is at the
> behest of the parent; in the second the child retains control (p. 123).
> The parallel with moral law founded in obedience to the Church,
> and that which is founded primarily in personal moral under-
> standing is obvious. 'When we control the alleviation of guilt in
> guilt-prone people we have considerable power over them. The hold
> that religion has on some people would seem to be based on this.'

False guilt can be very damaging. For example, parents whose
child turns out badly will certainly ask themselves what they did
wrong. They can attempt a clear-sighted evaluation of their
parenting and perhaps conclude that they were at fault and need not
have been, or that they did their best and accept that all parents
make mistakes, or that factors for which they had no responsibility
were the cause. But which is more likely to improve the outcome:

indulging in feelings of guilt for what cannot be helped, or exorcizing the baggage of guilt and getting on with tackling the constructive steps which may be open to them today?

Many sociologists and criminologists have identified low self-esteem as a major factor in criminal behaviour, and their regimes for the reformation of individuals contain a large element of rebuilding of self-esteem through increasing personal skills and offering the challenge of graded achievement to help their charges develop their pride and confidence. It is claimed that powerlessness to succeed in positive ways results in exercising power in negative ways, through various types of anti-social behaviour. But, well short of the criminal, we can see in ordinary people, including ourselves, how anxieties, fears and loss of sense of control can lead to inappropriate behaviour – a fact which any teacher will confirm from daily observation.

It is interesting that psychologists have identified a cluster of qualities in people who have high self-esteem. They tend to be confident, to have high self-respect, to view problems not as something unmanageable but as a challenge they can meet. They do not regard their failures as 'written in their stars' but as something for which they can take responsibility and about which they can do something constructive. They tend to be relaxed and they tend to be courteously mannered.[8]

It might be thought that high self-esteem would make a person not only conceited but also particularly blind to his own faults. However, the evidence is contrary. The criminologist knows that reform can only begin with the criminal recognizing the fault and taking responsibility for it. And I have noted how people with high rather than low self-esteem are able to own their failures, thus clearing the decks for positive action. Indeed the very process of owning failure (accepting that one has missed the mark) is in itself an achievement, boosting self-esteem in its own right.

What then of the Christian virtue of humility? Jesus is paradoxical about this and, as often in the Gospels, it is in the tension of the paradox that the truth can be found. He describes himself as lowly in heart (both the Douai and Jerusalem translations use the word 'humble'),[9] yet he is able to say that those who have seen him have seen the Father, and he is recognized as someone who speaks with authority. Jesus has high self-esteem, and his humility lies in recognizing that his power comes from the Father. He is powerful yet modest in his power for he acknowledges that he has been given it for a purpose. The moment we feel that the high value we place on ourselves is something that makes us intrinsically superior to others as a result of our own merits, humility turns into arrogance.

> At the age of 10 I became a religiously superior being. I accumulated Indulgences, I undertook lengthy penances, I spent much time at prayer. I began to feel that my school friends were spiritual laggards, destined for Hell or at least a very long period in Purgatory. I watched their inferior grasp of religious duties with a pharisaic eye. I must have been a very horrid little boy. Fortunately I began, dimly at first, to realize that something was going wrong. And before long I returned to the much healthier regime of a normal 10-year-old. I cannot say I have never been tempted by spiritual pride again but remembering this incident has triggered the alarm bells before it ever became more than a twinge.

Self-esteem is an over-arching pattern which in practice defines to a large extent what we are able to do. We are motivated to live up to the image we have of ourselves, or – unhappily – to live down to it. It also tends to be self-fulfilling. High self-esteem leads to high achievement and consequently grows; low self-esteem will be confirmed by the resulting low performance. But the right level of self-esteem is not always easy to acquire.

> In lecturing to sales people I have often drawn a large mouth on a flipchart to introduce the acronym LIPS. It means Limited Image Performance Syndrome. This marks the top and bottom boundaries within which an individual habitually performs. Sales results depend more on raising this than on any of the other myriad techniques which may be acquired. But the principle is universal.

For some people low self-esteem is a deep-set condition which they feel powerless to control. It can appear as a symptom of clinical depression or a recurrent tendency to depression, and may need professional treatment. Many others will benefit from the help of a counsellor who can midwife them through lesser difficulties. There are other possibilities such as assertiveness courses which can be beneficial – but they should be run by a reputable organization.

In the ordinary course of things self-esteem can be promoted first by understanding and grasping that it is a judgement we make about ourselves – which often bears little relationship to the real state of affairs. Two individuals with precisely similar qualities and skills can have very different levels of self-esteem. As Eleanor Roosevelt said: 'No one can make you feel inferior without your consent.' Dr Émile Coué used to teach his patients to recite the phrase 'Every day, in every way, I am getting better and better', repeatedly, night and morning, in order to slip positive feelings past the conscious barriers and into the unconscious. It may sound a bit trite, but the method is soundly based and effective.[10]

Second, we can choose whether to dwell on our failures or dwell on our successes. It can be valuable to spend a little time listing successes and then devise ways to keep these at the forefront of the mind.

> As a trivial example, when I find myself painting badly I look out such of my past pictures as were reasonable efforts, and take heart from the thought that once I could paint. More seriously, although my spiritual successes have been few enough I make the best of what I have in my memory to encourage me to feel better about myself.

One of the most useful methods is the nightly examination of conscience. I do not mean examination of conscience as it has usually been taught, where we attempt merely to list our sins. A proper examination of conscience must include a review of the ways in which we judge we have brought ourselves closer to God and our neighbour by our decisions and acts during that day. If it is true that loving acts improve our moral orientation then we should be consolidating this by thinking about what we have achieved, with God's help. Of course we look at our failures and accept them with sorrow but we can do more by focusing on what we can do to improve rather than by contemplating what we have done wrong. The evidence that this is more likely to lead to progress is strong. Similarly it is more effective to set ourselves concrete objectives than to have general aspirations towards improvement. Such objectives also give us clear ways in which we can judge our successes and so provide a motivating sense of achievement.[11]

Objectives need to be set with care. As far as possible they should be specific and measurable. And they must always be reasonable. It is easier to go upstairs step by step than to attempt one bound. Pope John Paul warns us not to mistake the gradual progress many of us make towards the moral law and the gradualness of the law itself.[12] He is of course using legal terminology here. In practice it is more constructive to focus on the next step on the stairs than to be continuously reminding ourselves of the ultimate objective. That is merely to encourage false guilt. We must hope that God will judge us all on our direction of travel rather than the precise step we have reached.

But a virtue is a habit. Achieving self-esteem is not a single objective; we have to maintain and increase it through practice, throughout our lives. The methods we apply require Practical Wisdom (Prudence) and the level we seek is monitored by Balance (Temperance). Our image of ourselves constantly varies against changing circumstances – adverse and positive, but we should search over time to have a sense of ourselves as someone who is important to God and can therefore do important things for him.

The Virtue of Empathy

This habit is closely connected to loving our neighbour since it requires us to be responsive to him as he is in himself and not merely as we see him from the outside. It should not be confused with sympathy (often good in itself but not relevant here) which means sharing our neighbour's feelings. Empathy means understanding what these feelings are so that we can react constructively to them.

> A hospital nurse will no doubt feel sympathy for her patients from time to time. However, she knows that she cannot afford to allow too much emotional involvement; this would not only be an unbearable strain for her but it could well interfere with her professional care. Yet if she is without empathy and so has no understanding of what her patients are feeling or experiencing then her ability to help them will be reduced.

Empathy preserves us from thinking that what is good for us will necessarily be good for our neighbour. This would be to love him as if he *were* ourselves. If we love him *as* we love ourselves then we have to try to love him in his own terms – from inside, so to speak. Only in this way can we love him in the way we love ourselves.

Imagine a situation – quite familiar nowadays – when you have finally reached a customer service clerk after a tedious track through an automated telephone system. How easy it is to allow your aggravation to colour your attitude to what you might see as non-cooperation. But think for a moment how it must feel to be the clerk, who is bound by the company's regulations and has spent the day, as he does every day, dealing with aggrieved customers.

Does the situation look a little different when we see it through the clerk's eyes? Is it possible that a better understanding of what the other person is experiencing would motivate us to be more constructive, and might even get us the help we require? As it happens telephone staff rate very low on job satisfaction; you might not care to change places with them except in your imagination.[13] I have chosen a relatively trivial example but the use of empathy extends over a very wide range. When your child tells you something – a triumph, a worry, a question – do you initially hear him from his point of view, the child's perspective? Your spouse comes back from a concert deeply moved by the performance. You are not musical but you can choose whether to acknowledge her pleasure in a casual way or you can try to see how the experience must have been for her.

Imagine some sexual disagreement between you; do both of you try to see the situation from each other's perspective? How easily are such problems solved without the virtue of empathy?

Empathy is needed everywhere. Subordinates often believe that their boss doesn't understand how it is for them, and the boss in turn often believes that his boss doesn't understand how it is for him. Symmetrically, bosses down the line each believe that they understand their subordinates very well.[14] Think what empathy could do here for happiness and effectiveness. Large-scale disputes, perhaps between unions and management, often find their source in a failure or an unwillingness to see how it is from the point of view of the other side. Christians are mandated to seek peace at every level between persons, and empathy is a first and necessary step to lasting peace.

Empathy is a virtue which descends from Fairness (Justice). One cannot be fair without giving full weight to the other person's point of view. And it requires Determination (Fortitude) because it is so much easier to slip back into our point of view than risk the discomfort of having to change one's mind.

The virtue of empathy does not come to most of us very easily. We are so bound up in ourselves and our reactions that we do not attend deeply to the reactions of others. Sometimes fear is a motivation. If you really try to see life from another's standpoint you are in danger of accepting that he has a level of right on his side – you might even end up in agreement, although empathy itself does not require this. I can empathize with a cannibal's belief that the only way to quell the revengeful spirits of his enemy is to eat him. But I do not have to agree that it is a good idea.

The virtue of empathy leads directly to the virtue of good manners. This does not of course mean social etiquette, although conforming to the reasonable social customs of the group lubricates social encounters. I have in mind sensitivity to others from understanding how it is for them. Irritation, curtness, lack of consideration are avoided, and our neighbour leaves our encounter feeling the better for it. Good manners might have prevented me from being curt to the telephone clerk simply because I had developed the habit of relating to others as I would like people to relate to me. Ironically we often show better manners to strangers than we do to those closer to us, suggesting that the habit is often motivated by our wish to appear a good person to others. So the test is whether we show good manners to those who know us too well to be fooled by our sudden assumption of courtesy for the sake of appearances. Of course being pleasing to others must be regulated by the more important virtues. Jesus did not employ good manners when he overturned the tables of the moneylenders in the Temple. So there will be occasions when in the interest of truth or right we have to be similarly firm, but we should still maintain courtesy as far as possible. Apart from its desirability in itself, courtesy, even – or particularly – when we express disagreement, makes it easier for our neighbour to listen to what we have to say.

When you start employing empathy in real life, and begin to respond to people as they experience themselves, you are likely to find that you are able to relate much more closely to them and, quite simply, to love them better. So empathy is a virtue which tends to reinforce itself. But there is always the temptation to lose the habit and return to our own egotistical point of view. However, there is another virtue closely related to empathy – in fact it is really a part of it. Because it is so demanding it deserves a section to itself.

The Virtue of Listening

So demanding? We all know the importance of listening, and of course we do listen. Not all the time, of course, but whenever it's appropriate. It's scarcely a virtue.

If you react like that you may be feeling like I did when I started my training as a marriage counsellor. My first discovery was that I was, contrary to my assumption, a very poor listener. Of course I heard what was said, I could even repeat its substance back quite accurately. But all the time I was interpreting and judging the speaker, and preparing myself for a response. Conversations were rather like a tennis rally – watching my opponent's shots so that I could get in a good return. I am not ashamed to confess it because unless you are an exception to the common run you are just the same.

Good listening is rare. It happens when the listener is focusing solely on the way in which the speaker is experiencing the situation, and not on the listener's own reaction to it. It is of course empathy put into action in the area of personal communication. Its value is completed when the speaker knows he has been listened to and deeply understood.

I have discussed the techniques of good listening elsewhere,[15] and I will not develop them in detail here. But you can start exploring how well you have been practising the virtue of listening quite easily.

The next time, and it may well be today, someone starts telling you something of importance to them – perhaps a colleague, perhaps a child, perhaps your spouse – try hearing what they say from their own perspective, looking at it with their emotional eyes. It is almost as if you were role-playing them as they speak. Leave your personal reactions – agreement, disagreement, helpful ideas, even pity – until later. Just now you are concerned only with understanding where the speaker is coming from. From time to time confirm in your own words what you think you have understood, resisting the temptation to interpret or comment. This not only sends the message that you really have been listening but also gives the speaker a chance to see what they have been saying and to correct or develop it if they wish. You will find the experience surprising and rewarding. But be prepared for longer conversations – this may be the first time the speaker has been truly listened to in his whole life, and he may never get another chance.

Good listening is difficult enough when you practise it deliberately. But a virtue is a habit and I at least found it extremely difficult to acquire. I had to remind myself continually to do it, and found it – and still find it – more difficult when my own emotions are involved. I find it easier when talking to friends, with their independent lives, than I do with my wife whose life I share.

It is possible to see listening as I have described it simply as a technique of social competence, and thus scarcely a virtue as such.

In fact it is rooted in, and promotes, respect for the other person and a recognition that they have a right to be fully heard. It is an office of love.

The Virtue of Recognizing Qualities

It is a sad comment on human nature that we are inclined to define people in terms of their defects and not in terms of their goodness. It is so much easier to see what people do wrong than what they do right, and our guardian devil is quick to remind us how much more fun it is. Which is the more accurate description: a list of a person's good qualities or a list of his defects? We certainly hope that God will have our qualities in the forefront of his mind when it comes to Judgement Day, so why should we do any less for our neighbour?

Of course one can get this out of balance (Temperance). There are times when negative criticism is called for, and may even be a duty, but the virtue of recognizing qualities first and defects a reluctant second, if at all, is important to cultivate. Jesus was as aware as his friends of the lifestyle of the woman who anointed his feet, but what he saw first and predominantly was her love – and the rest didn't matter.[16]

Acquiring the habit of instinctively looking to see the good in others first and foremost shows us the work of God in many surprising places – because good, even when partial or mangled, finds its source in God. Honour among thieves may be unsatisfactory but it is a scintilla reflecting – however imperfectly – the honour of God. We have become so accustomed to thinking in terms of sin and of our lower natures that we can forget that man was created to rise, that goodness is the true purpose of his nature. Many years of counselling taught me that people have a basic orientation towards the good; my more humble job was simply to help them clear away the obstacles which prevented that good from coming to full maturity. I saw my client as a cork in a bucket naturally seeking the surface but artificially held down by the rubbish of sin and error and circumstance. Before a counselling session I would pray to the Holy Spirit to help me in obstacle-clearing; but the major work of the Holy Spirit was the internal motivation of the client to find his way upwards.

The recognition of good qualities draws us closer to our neighbour, and enables us to respond to him in more fruitful ways. And, as I have already noted, people are much more motivated to work at increasing their good qualities than at eradicating their bad ones. If they do so the bad will often quietly disappear: 'Therefore I tell you her sins, which are many, are forgiven, for she loved much.'

The Virtue of Autonomy

I have described autonomy in Chapter 2, and have made appropriate reference to the central part it plays in the moral life. In summary I repeat the passage from *Gaudium et Spes*: the purpose of this freedom is that through its exercise man is able to 'spontaneously seek his creator and by cleaving to him perfect himself so as to be ready for heaven. Man's dignity then demands that he should act in accordance with a free and conscious choice, personally, inwardly persuaded, and not by either blind impulse from within or coercion from without.'[17] Autonomy, then, is at the heart of Christian growth.

The virtue of autonomy as I describe it is concerned with the habit of freely making personal decisions and being ready to act on them. It is not for everyone an easy habit to acquire because we seem to have an inbuilt inclination towards obedience; a large part of us says that we don't want to make decisions which we then have to stand by. We'd rather someone told us what to do, then we feel safe.

Society, whether human or animal, can only avoid chaos if there are a few leaders and a large number of followers. Since chaotic societies do not survive it is likely that our instinctive response to authority is an evolutionary adaptation. This was dramatically confirmed by Professor Stanley Milgram's famous 1963 experiments at Yale University in which subjects were required by ostensible authority to give increasing electric shocks to pseudo-subjects – who were in fact collaborators with the investigators.[18] The subjects were told that it was an experiment into the effects of punishment and learning. Two interesting facts emerged. One was that it was predicted by competent people before the experiment began that only 2 or 3 per cent of the subjects would be 'obedient'. The second was that in fact every subject turned out to be willing to inflict shocks of 240 volts at the imprecations of the clinically coated authority – despite the howls and groans of their victims, and many were prepared to go to the maximum of 450 volts. The experiments were reproduced by other psychologists and with diverse groups – such as men versus women, different racial backgrounds, religious versus non-religious. Substantially similar results were reported.

Interestingly – but not surprisingly for that time – Catholics were found to be somewhat more conformist than Jews or Protestants. It seems that not only do we, and I must include myself, have a strong instinct to obey authority but also that we are largely unaware of it. Milgram commented: 'If an anonymous experimenter could successfully command adults to subdue a 50-year-old man and force on him painful electric shocks against his protests, one can only wonder what government, with its vastly greater authority and prestige, can command of its subjects.' If you imagine that the Germans were ready to obey their evil orders in World War II because they had some gene which made them compliant by nature you are correct. But it was by human nature not by German nature, and there, but for the Grace of God, go I. And if you are not ready to stand beside me then you are the more dangerous; at least I acknowledged my instinct – and am therefore motivated to cultivate the virtue which can keep it under control.[19]

While it is easy to see how this tendency was widespread among Catholics in the mid-twentieth century, how does this square with the more recent general rejection of the Church's moral authority which I have documented? Sadly, it confirms its depths. The obedience instinct only operates when the authority is credible; once abandoned it loses its power. Though even here the latent instinct in our genes can maintain a sense of vestigial guilt. And of course there is a substantial minority of Catholics who believe that the strictest adherence to the most uncompromising authority is a consummation devoutly to be wished. Only the individual can hope to decide to what extent the instinct inherited from his sub-hominid ancestors contributes to this conclusion, though Milgram suggests that it is possible that he will underestimate its effect substantially. But the coin has another side: were the Church's true authority to regain credibility then the instinct to respond to recognized leadership would be a powerful ally.

However, one should not assume that those who reject orthodox teaching are necessarily exercising a thoughtful autonomy. It is only too easy for rejection to become an end in itself – as though dissent were in some way an expression of adulthood. Instead of being based on reason, our criteria can become what *we* want, or the questionable values of the group in which we move, or the values of society in general. We may lose any sense of objective law – which makes us free – and become slaves to the criteria of the false gods. We do not lose our instinctive response to authority, we merely substitute, often unconsciously, a new set of authorities.

The virtue of autonomy requires us to develop and maintain the active habit of questioning everything which is presented to us as something we ought to do and trying to make a sincere judgement of reason about it. In later chapters I shall be discussing this process in looking at how conscience may be correctly formed, but here I want to look at practical ways of developing habitual autonomy.

Because of the deep instinct to obedience I have described, because of our fears, and because of our laziness it is an uphill task. We may have to take strong steps to get the process moving. I think of our natural tendencies as being like a warped stick; it may be necessary to bend it back past the centre in order to end up straight. The first check is whether or not the authority is legitimate – has this individual the actual authority he claims? And does his authority extend to the matter in hand? Petty officialdom is given to making up its own rules for its own convenience and it often seems easier to comply than to question. Is the requirement a reasonable one, and being exercised reasonably for the common good? Is it appropriate in the precise circumstances of its occurring? Is obedience going to cause more harm than good? And that could include harm or inconvenience to ourselves. Are we simply assuming that authority exists, and blindly taking our place in the sheep flock when the dog isn't there? I am not advocating the barrack room lawyer; the individual who goes 'agin the government' on principle is as enslaved as the compliant wimp. In most cases the answers to these questions will result in intelligent obedience, but the possibility that they may not must be constantly borne in mind. But I am advocating that, because we are warped in the direction of obedience, we must work habitually to develop an internal bias towards freedom and intelligent choice. It will not always be popular and we may occasionally have to pay a penalty for our autonomy. A modern phrase exhorts us to 'go with the flow' but the Christian needs to ask where the flow is going, and whether he should be swimming upstream.

> The subjects in the Milgram experiment were volunteers, free to abandon the task at any time. Yet they imputed such authority to the 'experimenter' that they did not question his right to order them to administer to another innocent volunteer (as they thought) what amounted to severe torture. Any more of course than the executioner questioned the authority of Church and State when he applied the torch to the faggots that were to burn the Protestants in the reign of Mary Tudor.

When I wrote about this deep human need to obey (*Tablet*, 30 May 1981) I suggested that it would be prudent to cultivate the virtue of 'Christian disobedience', to counter it. This does not yet appear in the Catechism amongst the list of virtues, but perhaps it should – as a subsection of autonomy. As Ralph Waldo Emerson said in his *Politics*: 'Good men must not obey the laws too well.'

The Virtue of Respect for Others' Autonomy

If we take the virtue of recognizing good qualities in others, and add to it the virtue of autonomy, then put the mixture into the framework of loving our neighbour as ourselves, we arrive at the virtue of respecting the autonomy of others. This is centred on a habit of mind which holds that we would always prefer others to increase their autonomy rather than to inhibit their autonomy in the interests of what we, with our superior knowledge, know is good for them.

The virtue is hard to cultivate because our instinct to help other people is rightly strong. We want to tell them about, even direct them into, behaviour from which they will benefit, and for which, no doubt, they will thank us. It is hard to sit back and let them get on with their responsibilities. It is also hard because it requires the continual judgement of practical wisdom (Prudence). Parenthood may be described as the art of managing separation. From a status of complete dependence the child moves to an adult status of independence. At each stage the parent has to decide just how much responsibility to allow to the child. Too much, too early, is dangerous. Too little, too late, can lead to revolt or to a child having to take adult decisions without having been prepared for the task. Similarly when we have responsibility for others in the workplace or in other authority relationships we must continually judge the right point at which to increase their autonomy.

However, practitioners of this virtue instinctively favour the least interference with the autonomy of others consistent with the responsibility they actually have for them. Their wish is to free people to exercise their own autonomy, and grow with its exercise. They continually ask themselves the question: 'Is this my problem to solve or is it someone else's problem?' And they let the problem rest with its proper owner.

I shall return in due course to how this virtue may be applied in the exercise of authority within hierarchical institutions.

The Virtue of Social Independence

This virtue should perhaps be a further subsection of autonomy. Let me illustrate it:

A newspaper cartoon showed a stalled car being fiercely hooted by the car behind. The driver of the stalled car walks sweetly over and she says: 'Why don't you start my car while I hoot your horn?'

I hope I am not the only person who has been rattled by pressure from another driver, and even done something thoughtless or potentially dangerous as a result. Most of us fear social embarrassment and, taken unawares, unlike the driver in the cartoon, we can be hustled into an unwise action. In such situations the pressure is immediate and strong; we even have a distinct physiological reaction to it. In other situations the pressure of the group to conform is similarly powerful. Both the words 'ethics' and 'morals' come from roots which mean customs or habits, and a pre-Christian view might be that your first duty is to follow the customs of your community. In one sense this is true: if we live in a community we have a general duty to be a supportive member and abide by its rules. But a Christian must ultimately derive his judgements from his perception of the truth; the values of the community cannot be directly a source of truth, though they may witness to it. The psychologists who have tracked moral development in children suggest that the move from deriving moral imperatives from the community to holding imperatives derived independently and potentially at variance with the community comes at quite a late stage of maturity; and many adults never succeed in making this jump.

The pressures to conform to group values are extremely strong at the psychological level, as you would expect from a tendency bred in our genes. Numerous experiments have been conducted that confirm this in a variety of circumstances.

One of the more dramatic experiments, conducted at Stanford University, involved a group of men who were arbitrarily divided into 'Guards' and 'Prisoners', under simulated prison conditions. Within a very short time the 'Guards' began to take on brutal characteristics in their role and the 'Prisoners' began to show symptoms of physical and emotional distress. The experiment had to be stopped prematurely in order to avoid psychological damage.[20]

Other experiments have shown how people can be manipulated to change their group loyalties, or even to disbelieve the clear evidence of their own eyes under pressure from the group. It seems that we need the group as a reference point – we feel safe when we decide in concert with others, and we feel uncomfortable in facing antagonism from a group to which we belong but to which we do not conform. In this context it is interesting that the spell of social pressure is more easily broken when others have refused to conform before us. This suggests that breakaway movements such as those current in the Church spread like a kind of infection. In fact one may even come to conform with a new group – the group of those who do not conform.

Group and community pressures also have the power of being very positive. We are often urged to keep good company, and this is wise because we are then employing social pressure as a support to our values. But they must be *our* values, so part of us has always to stand aside and verify the group's values before accepting them. This is equally true for our membership of the Church community. It is no secret that there have been many periods in history when general attitudes of the Church have been simply at variance with the Gospel. Fortunately the Judeao-Christian tradition has been studded with prophets, major and minor, who have called for reform. Few of us can claim that title but at least we can retain our autonomy in our own judgements.

This may not be easy because the evidence suggests that the more strongly we are linked into the group the more we replace our individual personality with the group personality. As Emerson said: 'Society everywhere is in conspiracy against the manhood of every one of its members' (*Self-Reliance*).

So the virtue of social independence is hard to acquire. Once again we have to seek opportunities to develop and practise it so that it is in full working order when we need it.

Summary

My first consideration in this chapter was the emphasis which has been traditionally laid on becoming morally oriented people through the development and practice of the virtues. Much of the debate today on the resolution of contentious moral questions can distract us from this more important task. Having summarized the categories of virtues as they are customarily considered I have described certain virtues, not usually listed, which seem to be important to acquire in order to form ourselves as moral people, and to help us make the right moral judgements when we encounter them.

The virtue of self-esteem develops our ability to love ourselves as a base for loving others. It is a first step in being able to take responsibility for what we do or have done. And through it we counter the paralysing temptation of false guilt. From the respect we have for ourselves comes our ability to respect others, and the virtue of empathy strengthens the habit of seeing others through their own eyes so that we can be truly responsive to them – we love our neighbours as we love ourselves, from within. The virtue of listening is the habit through which we most often exercise empathy in our relations with others. The virtue of recognizing qualities addresses our habitual way of judging others – do we see them primarily in terms of their good qualities or bad? Do we judge them as we ourselves would wish to be judged?

The major virtue of autonomy is enjoined on us by Pope and Council; through it we exercise our judgements of the good through our reason and thereby conform ourselves to the will of God. It is exercised within the law, although there may be conflicts as to what the law actually requires. Autonomy may lead us into formal disobedience to authority for the sake of obedience to the good as we responsibly judge it. Related to this and to our recognition of others' qualities is the virtue of respecting their autonomy. An attendant virtue is that of social independence through which we maintain enough distance from the communities in which we live to verify their values no matter how strong the pressure to conform may be.

This selection of virtues does not pretend to be complete, and they are exercised in the spirit of the hinge virtues: Practical Wisdom (Prudence), Fairness (Justice), Determination (Fortitude) and Balance (Temperance). And all of these are linked to and are governed by the Christian virtues of Faith, Hope and Charity. And the greatest of these is Charity.

Notes to Chapter 4

1. Rom. 7.19.
2. *Veritatis Splendor* 71.
3. The relationship between the 'fundamental option' of the individual towards God and the effect of specific moral acts on that option is currently under dispute. Fortunately it is not relevant here, but those interested may like to look at section 65ff. in *Veritatis Splendor* and 'The Theory of the Fundamental Option and Moral Action' by Thomas R. Kopfensteiner, in *Christian Ethics*, ed. Bernard Hoose, (Continuum, 1998).
4. See for instance *Catechism of the Catholic Church* 1. 7 (Chapman) or a modern and discursive account in Charles E. Curran, *The Catholic Moral Tradition Today* (Georgetown University Press, 1999).
5. *Summa Theologica* II I 55.4.
6. 1 Cor. 13.3.
7. Rom. 5.8.
8. I review the evidence and its effect in secular situations in my *How to Get Your Own Way in Business* (Gower, 1990), *passim*.
9. Rom. 11.29.
10. *De la suggestion et de ses applications* (1915).
11. H. H. Meyer, E. Kay and J. R. French, Jr, 'Split Roles in Performance Appraisal', *Harvard Business Review* (January 1965).
12. Homily at the close of the Sixth Synod of Bishops (25 October 1980), and referred to, in the context of married couples responding to the prohibition of contraception, in *Familiaris Consortio* (1981), sec. 34.

13. Economic and Social Research Council study on job satisfaction in several professions, reported in *The Times* (3 September 1999).

14. Some studies are summarized in Charles Handy, *Understanding Organizations* (Penguin, 1981).

15. *Managing People and Problems* (Gower, 1988).

16. Luke 7.

17. *Veritatis Splendor* 38 ff; *Gaudium et Spes* 17.

18. S. Milgram, 'Behavioral Study of Obedience', *Journal of Abnormal and Social Psychology*, 67 (1963), pp. 371–8.

19. It is ironic that Milgram mounted his experiments to give himself a baseline in order to investigate whether Germans had a racial tendency to obedience. But the tendency turned out not to be German racial but human racial. Dr Jack Dominian has written about psychological aspects of conformity in his *Authority* (Burns & Oates, 1976).

20. See C. Haney, C. Banks and P. Zimbardo, *International Journal of Criminology and Penology*, 1 (1973), pp. 69–97. Most basic textbooks on social psychology contain accounts of social conformity as established by experiment. For instance K. Deaux and L. S. Wrightsman, *Social Psychology* (California: Brooks/Cole Publishing Company, 1988).

CHAPTER 5

FALLIBLE AND INFALLIBLE

In Chapter 2 I described the third element of conscience as the practical application of its basic principles to the judgements we have to make or have made. The objective is to discern the truth – that is, the good which is found in the correspondence of the action with human nature as God created it. This process is known as the formation of conscience. Reason tells us that we have an obligation to form it in a way which is adequate to the matter in hand, taking into account the time available if it is urgent. It follows that to fail to seek the truth makes our justification empty of worth.

Formation of conscience is a central theme in this book because, as I say in my Introduction, I perceive a vacuum caused by the Church's failure to develop and teach and advocate the proper formation of conscience. The consequence of this is that there is a widespread tendency towards an untutored do-it-yourself formation which relies heavily on an untethered autonomy and, in many instances, is no more than consulting one's own preferences.

Formed by the Church?

Some would say that the formation of the Catholic conscience is a relatively simple matter on the grounds that since the major starting point of conscience formation is the Church's extensive moral teaching the criteria are provided for us, and all that is left is to decide whether or not a particular law applies in a particular case. And in a number of instances we do not even have to do that because some actions are evil of their own nature and consequently cannot be justified by other circumstances. To put it simply: you have to form your conscience; and you do this by discovering what the Church teaches, together with its comprehensive network of guidance as to how it all should be applied. Lo! your conscience is formed.

> In the early 1960s I proposed that the entire network of Catholic moral teachings and application should be computerized. The system seemed to me so comprehensive that one might simply feed in a moral dilemma and receive a complete solution. I notice that Greg Garvey of Concordia University, Montreal, has proposed, I trust in the same spirit of irony, a computer confessional housed in an automatic teller machine. In brief, each sin has a weighting according to gravity and is multiplied by the number of occurrences. The ATM processes the input, calculates the amount and form of penance, and produces absolution.[1]
>
> In the *Tablet* of 7 July 2001 there is a short report of a polyglot list of sins for the use of tourists in Marbella enabling the penitent to point to sins in his own language, and the confessor to read it in his. There is a corresponding polyglot list of penances and no doubt the form of absolution to which the *digitus sacerdotis* can point in response. Subsequently it was reported that such lists go back until at least 1940, and no doubt earlier examples exist.

Of course this is a caricature of the part that the Church's moral teaching should play in conscience formation although, having received my moral education in the middle of the twentieth century, it was the impression with which I was left. And the description Father Davis gave of how it should be conducted (Chapter 3) suggests why this should have been so.

The Council document *Gaudium et Spes* says: 'Man's dignity then demands that he should act in accordance with a free and conscious choice, personally, inwardly persuaded, and not by either blind impulse from within or coercion from without.' The statement is plain and unqualified. But in a later passage, when referring to how a married couple should execute their decision to limit their families, it says: 'They must be guided by conscience, and conscience must be conformed to the divine law; they must submit to the Church's teaching authority which interprets the law authoritatively by the light of the Gospel.'[2] In *Dignitatis Humanae*, the decree on religious liberty, the Council says: 'However, in forming their conscience, Christians must pay careful attention to the holy and sacred teachings of the Church[3] ... For by Christ's will the Catholic Church is the teacher of truth; it is her task to declare and teach authentically the truth which is Christ. She also has to use her authority to expound the principles of the moral order which stem from the actual nature of men.'[4] Pope John Paul draws on this last passage in *Veritatis Splendor*.

This has all the ring of parents who, having let their child run free, suddenly panic and run after him with a leading rein. Freedom is fine in theory, until the child starts to use it. The effect of this dissonance is to achieve the strange result of allowing its members a conscience which is both bound and free at the same time. A good trick if you can do it.

It is important to face up to this dilemma. In real life the number of occasions where the Church's absolutist teaching plays a substantial part are very few, yet the possibility is always there and is inevitably encountered from time to time. In this chapter I shall try to show how a proper response to the Church's authority first distinguishes between infallible teachings and teachings which are not infallible. Infallible teachings, in so far as they exist at present in the moral sphere, only bind because we freely, and in conscience, accept the Church as true. We are not only at liberty to reject her but actually obliged to do so if we do not believe this. Non-infallible teachings are taught with the Church's authority and therefore require appropriate deference – as the teaching of any other lawful authority does. Her non-infallible moral teachings vary in their gravity but none require the assent of Faith, and all of them require validation through the judgement of conscience. Validation normally comes from us seeing for ourselves, often with the help of the reasons given by the Church, that the teaching conforms with the demands of love. But in some instances where we are uncertain, validation comes through accepting that the Church is more likely to have identified the truth than us.

The principles arising out of this distinction are orthodox. If they appear radical it is because they are not always given the prominence that they deserve. But the balance has changed. It used to be thought that occasions when a Catholic might be justified in rejecting a teaching would not only be few and far between but would require the careful judgement of an individual well qualified to consider all the factors. Moreover all the favourable assumptions had to be on the side of the Magisterium, and the risk of disagreement was always grave – a man was betting his eternal future against his conscience. The change of balance has come about first because there is a greater realization based on history that the Magisterium has in fact sometimes been wrong in its serious moral teachings, and rather frequently wrong in the general atmosphere and emphasis of the moral attitudes it has encouraged. Connected with this has been a tendency for the Magisterium to allow the law as witness to love to become law as the *de facto* objective of morality. Reverting to love as the true objective has provided a criterion against which the law, as it has been developed, is sometimes found wanting. Secondly, a much better informed and educated laity – able to see the arguments laid out for them by specialists – are in a better position to make judgements which they are entitled to trust. It is still the case that to go against the Magisterium's serious teaching should be exceptional, but it has become a real, rather than a mainly theoretical, possibility for the ordinary Catholic.

To say that the Church has been sometimes wrong in respect of its moral teachings is not intended as a criticism. It is inevitable that the Magisterium, like an ordinary individual, must make its judgements according to its present lights and knowledge. And of course there will be actions which were appropriate in the conditions of society at a past time which are not appropriate now; in the nature of things this may result in an *ad hoc* teaching achieving the apparent status of irreformability. My criticism is directed only against the Church's unwillingness to accept and acknowledge that its view of moral demands can in many instances only be provisional. Its failure to do so makes reform in the light of greater understanding long delayed and requires an ingenuity in demonstrating that a new teaching is only a development rather than a change; this, in turn, brings its intellectual integrity into disrepute. I argue that there is a pressing need for making the public case for reform when this seems called for; the time for keeping such dissent inside the closet is now past.

The Infallible and the Fallible

The first step is to distinguish between the teachings which are infallible and those which are not. I am not concerned at this point with which teaching falls into which category but simply to consider the characteristics of the two categories.[5]

The teachings regarded as infallible relate to the declaration of the First Vatican Council where the power to teach morals with absolute authority was asserted. It is in fact a rather empty category; there seems to be general agreement that no moral teachings have been so defined, except those intrinsically connected with the nature of the Sacraments. And in the light of the Canon Law principle that no doctrine is understood to have been defined infallibly unless this fact is manifest (Can. 749), the application of this category is not yet relevant. It has sometimes been a close thing. There were powerfully placed champions who argued that *Humanae Vitae* should be declared infallible, and references to infallibility in relation to morals were only excised from *Veritatis Splendor* at the last moment.[6] So we may not have long to wait. A future infallible pronouncement may well be imperfect in its articulation and may then be developed in a 'forward direction', to use Karl Rahner's phrase, but so far as it goes its acceptance is a condition of being a Catholic. This does not amount to a conscience being bound and free at the same time because the judgement of conscience that an infallible teaching is in error is *ipso facto* a judgement that the Church does not have the ultimate protection of the Holy Spirit. Thus it cannot be the true Church. It would be interesting to speculate on the state of the Church today if *Humanae Vitae* had been declared infallible. Perhaps a loophole would have been found.

The encyclical on the ordination of women, *Ordinatio Sacerdotalis* (1994), was subsequent to its publication ruled to be infallible by the

Congregation for the Doctrine of the Faith (CDF) on the basis that it was the constant and common teaching of the Magisterium, but since a Congregation itself is not infallible, notwithstanding the Pope's agreement to the ruling, theologians have argued that a necessary link in the chain is missing.[7]

It does not follow that there are no moral principles held as certainly true by virtue of our own and the community's recognition of their truth. As examples, the Ten Commandments enshrine general principles which we accept, although the application of some of them in particular instances requires some hard thinking. The Council focuses on offences against human life and the dignity of man.[8] Behind this there is a prevailing belief in the unique value of the individual who should always be treated as an end and never as a means to an end. The *Catechism of the Catholic Church* gives blasphemy, perjury, murder and adultery as always wrong, irrespective of the circumstances (para. 1756). A cursory glance at the secular world in its political, business, social and individual spheres reveals how much of this is either ignored or being gradually attenuated almost out of existence.

Accepting an infallible teaching on the Church's authority does not excuse us from working hard at understanding its meaning and the reasons behind it. The more clearly we can see the truth for ourselves and explore it the more closely we are conformed to God.

Fallible Teachings

The remainder of the Magisterium's moral teachings are not infallible. Or, to remove the double negative, they are fallible. They are not nearly infallible or more infallible than some other doctrine – just as something cannot be nearly or more unique. It is either the one or the other. (Of course a doctrine may be hybrid, when it has an infallible and a non-infallible element, but this complication does not affect the principle.) This is not only a demand of logic; it is a matter of history. As Karl Rahner puts it 'many doctrines which were once universally held have proved to be problematic or erroneous'.[9] Examples quoted usually include usury, universally held to be wrong in the early Church and condemned by more than one council. Slavery, although mitigated by the Magisterium, was condoned for many centuries, and even the 1913 *Catholic Encyclopaedia* felt unable to declare that it was against the natural law. Yet Pope John Paul, drawing on *Gaudium et Spes,* specifies slavery as one of the acts which are evil in themselves. The *Encyclopaedia* tells us that the positive suppression of heresy by ecclesiastical and civil authority is as old as the Church. Torture in the process of the Inquisition was authorized by papal bulls. The death sentence for heresy was officially carried out by the State, but it was specifically accepted as a condign punishment by Pope Gregory IV. It is hard to square this with *Dignitatis Humanae* (3) which teaches: 'He [man] must not be forced to act in any way against his conscience. Nor must he be prevented from acting according to his conscience, particularly in religious matters.' When the Pope tells the assembled ambassadors that the Holy See 'has always been vigorous in defending freedom of conscience and religious liberty',[10] I think of his predecessor, Pius IX, condemning the proposition 'Every man is free to embrace and profess that religion which, guided by the light of reason, he shall consider true.'[11]

While apologia are sometimes provided, attempting to show a consistency or 'forward' development in the change from the old teaching to the new, these often seem to owe more to ingenuity than to the plain facts. We suffer throughout the ages from a chronocentric[12] tendency which leads us to assume that, although we may have misunderstood an issue in the past, our current understanding will endure. What matters here is that serious positions once held generally by Catholics and sustained by teaching authority are now recognized as wrong. So we must accept that non-infallible teachings current today may in some instances be recognized as wrong in the future, just as some have in the past.

The Free Conscience Responding to the Magisterium

However, strictly speaking, examples are not needed. The fallibility of any teaching precludes its ability to bind consciences without qualification. Because it may be wrong it is necessary for me to make a judgement about whether I am able to validate it. Validation may come in two ways. The first is through the verification of my reason – the ordinary faculty through which conscience operates. The second is by validation through my acceptance that this matter, about which I am in doubt, is one on which the Magisterium is better qualified to judge. An analogy may help:

> Imagine that I have a child who is given to bed-wetting. I consult a doctor who advises that psychoanalysis is the appropriate route to cure. If I am ignorant of the subject it would be prudent of me to take the advice because it is likely that he knows more than I. But if I am familiar with the literature which establishes that behavioural rather than psychoanalytic methods are effective I must reject his advice because I should seek the good of my child. Furthermore I have a knowledge which a therapist cannot have: I know my child. So I must bring this into the equation before judging how I should proceed.

Essentially the analogy holds. I must use the best way open to me in order to establish the truth. Accepting the Magisterium's teaching as the best way in certain instances is appropriate though it may lack the benefits of moral growth which autonomous verification would give me. I described this earlier as 'an exercise of diminished autonomy'. But ideally I would hope and expect that the reasons proposed by the Magisterium for its teaching would convince or confirm me, just as reasons given by the doctor might.

The analogy is not perfect because the Church, unlike the doctor, has received her mission to teach from Christ and is sustained in this by the Holy Spirit. Since I am weighing the fallible judgement of my conscience against the fallible judgement of a Church supported by this mandate and protection ought I not to accept that the burden of proof lies with me and that I have an obligation in practice always to follow the more credible authority? But there is a difficulty here. In many moral matters I am trying to make a choice between two evils. For example if I had received an instruction to seek out heretics in line with Papal exhortations to extirpate heresy but judged that this conflicted with their personal rights, should I have put the Magisterium's judgement against mine? If I am a migrant worker returning for a brief holiday with my wife who happens at that time to be fertile should I forgo the sexual expression of our married love for another year because it would be dangerous for her to be pregnant? Am I damned if I do and divorced if I don't? I cannot escape the obligation to make a judgement and then do what I believe is right.

With Added 'Holy Spirit . . .'

No one has greater need of the help of the Holy Spirit than I, and it is help which I often feel I have received. But I do not justify my decisions on the grounds of his inspiration – I need to justify them through my natural faculties. I accept that the Church is preserved by the Holy Spirit from error in infallible matters and that his general guidance supports the Church. But when he is invoked as support for specific non-infallible matters I demur. Was the Spirit there when John XXIII was elected? But how about Alexander VI? As Cardinal Ratzinger said on Bavarian television: 'It would be a mistake to believe that the Holy Spirit picks the pope because there are too many examples of popes the Holy Spirit would obviously not have chosen.' He said the Spirit leaves considerable room for the free exercise of human judgement, probably guaranteeing only that, in the end, the Church will not be ruined.[13] The good priests of my parish were no doubt called by the Spirit but how about the paedophile priest? Was the Spirit behind the Inquisition, and also behind the Council declaration on religious liberty? Was the Spirit behind Pope St Gregory the Great when he said that married sexual intercourse could not in practice be performed without sin, or behind the Council's statement that it must be honoured with great reverence? Since on some occasions he may be present and on others he is apparently not, and we have no way of knowing which, there is a problem. Until some good evidence can be produced of his presence in a specific matter it seems to be no more than a kind of superstitious magic to bolster a case by claiming his support. Like me the Magisterium has to go through the ordinary processes of judgement, and then observe the fruits. Claiming a further buttress in the Holy Spirit suggests a lack of confidence in the evidence for the teaching. It might be better to employ the humility Bernard Shaw put into Joan of Arc's mouth (*mutatis mutandis*) when she was asked if she were in a state of Grace: 'If I do not have the Holy Spirit may God bring him to me: if I have, may God keep him with me.'

> History is studded with examples of men ascribing their triumphs or defeats to the will of God. The Elizabethans put the defeat of the Armada down to the will of God; the Puritans under Cromwell similarly recognized his hand in the winning of the battle of Marston Moor. The will of God has frequently been used as an excuse both by Christianity and by other religions for committing atrocities. This taking of God's name in vain, instead of using our best efforts and humbly hoping he is with us, are instances of fundamentalism as I describe it in Chapter 2. Sadly the Catholic Church is not immune.

Two Kinds of Authority

In my endeavour to describe the limitations of non-infallible teachings I must not be taken as minimizing the importance of the Church's authority as a moral teacher. Kevin Kelly suggests, subject to discussion, what seems to me a useful distinction. When the Church is handing on the living word of God through infallible teaching she is handing on his message, not her own; although she chooses the words through which to speak it we can be sure that it is God we hear. Where non-infallible teachings are given she also has authority – but it is a 'delegated' authority to teach her own message which is her understanding of what God demands; we hear the human institution speaking in virtue of this authority but doing so subject to the imperfections and limitations of the human condition.[14] This delegated authority is given to her by Christ and is exercised in many ways. In fact in the nature of things it covers the vast bulk of what she teaches and the regulations she makes. The use of her infallibility is exceptional – and typically exercised when some matter connected with Revelation is in doubt. One occasionally gets the impression from current writings that without the note of infallibility a teaching may be virtually ignored.

The Church puts this rather more strongly. She interprets the law authoritatively by the light of the Gospel (see above) and so her members 'must submit to the Church's teaching'. And she uses phrases like 'adhere with religious submission of will and intellect to the teachings which either the Roman Pontiff or the College of Bishops enunciate when they exercise their authentic Magisterium'.[15] I am not sure how one submits to a teaching, unless 'teaching' is a euphemism for law. The religious submission of the will and intellect is also a strange phrase. No one may will something which he sees as wrong and no one can force the intellect away from the truth as it discerns it. And if both will and intellect already adhere through autonomous judgement then the whole phrase seems otiose. As the Vatican II decree *Dignitatis Humanae* says: 'The truth cannot impose itself except by virtue of its own truth, as it makes its entrance into the mind at once quietly and with power.' But I am being disingenuous; I know what these phrases are generally taken to mean. I would just prefer them to be written in accurate language.

I would paraphrase my understanding of the position as follows. Given the Church's authority from Christ to teach morals, all her members are obliged to come to her non-infallible teachings not merely with an open mind but with a genuine desire to study and understand them so that they may accept them with the assent of their will and intellect. It follows from the imperative of truth as we see it that if they conclude – following examination commensurate with the degree of authority behind the teaching – that it would be wrong to accept it, then they are obliged in conscience to reject it.[16]

There should be nothing to frighten the horses in this; it reflects the established position. Cardinal Newman, in his *Letter to the Duke of Norfolk*, demonstrates with the clarity of a historian and a scholar the right of conscience to reject authoritative teaching in 'extreme' cases. Such cases do not qualify: 'Unless a man is able to say to himself, as in the Presence of God, that he must not, and dare not, act upon the Papal injunction, he is bound to obey it, and would commit a great sin in disobeying it.' The *Catholic Encyclopedia* (1913), in its article on infallibility, says:

> But if one believes in the objectivity of eternal and immutable truth, he will find it difficult to reconcile with a worthy conception of the Divine attributes a command under penalty of damnation to give unqualified and irrevocable internal assent to a large body of professedly Divine doctrine the whole of which is possibly false ... internal assent is obligatory only on those who can give it consistently with the claims of objective truth on their conscience – this conscience, it is assumed, being directed by a spirit of generous loyalty to genuine Catholic principles.

In 1967 the German Bishops addressed the question of disagreement with non-infallible teachings. While making it clear that to refuse assent was always a serious matter and that one would have to be ready to defend the sincerity of one's search on Judgement Day, they admit its possibility in principle. The following year they had to convert this from theory to practice in response to *Humanae Vitae*. Referring to their previous letter they said:

> In that letter we did not exclude the possibility that a Catholic might hold, on serious grounds, he should deviate from an ecclesiastical decision which falls outside the scope of infallibility. Many conscientious Catholics, priest and layman, are evidently convinced that this is the case as regards methods of birth control. As always in this matter the need for consciences to be formed demands of us that mere subjective feelings must be overcome and that we should be prepared to examine our consciences critically. On the other hand, a responsible decision made in conscience must be respected by all.

If the influence of the Church or of the times has led to deficiencies in conduct, in Church discipline, or even in the formulation of doctrine (which must be carefully distinguished from the deposit of faith) these should be appropriately rectified at the proper moment. I have cheated here by not using inverted commas; in fact this sentence is a direct quote from the Council decree of Ecumenism *Unitatis Redintegratio,* as translated in Abbott (para 6).[17] Abbott's footnote reads: 'It is remarkable, indeed, for an Ecumenical Council to admit the possible deficiency of previous doctrinal formulations.' But it should not be remarkable for the Council to refer to the well-established facts. I presume that Abbott's surprise arose because a dangerous truth long kept in the background had suddenly been brought into the light of day.

These statements, and many others like them, differ in the rigour they apply to the withholding of assent, but they agree on the central principle. In fact teachings are given with various degrees of authority and the level of rigour appropriate to each degree will apply, bearing in mind the division in kind rather than degree between the infallible and the fallible.

Christian Scepticism

I suggested in Chapter 4 that in cultivating the virtue of autonomy it is important to bear in mind our deep, and often unconscious, bias towards obedience – and that one might have to take strong steps to overcome this bias. Consequently I would advocate a habitual attitude of interrogation towards the moral law as presented. We have to be prepared to go against the grain of natural deferential obedience in order to confirm the teaching as far as we can. For example the encyclical *Evangelium Vitae* (1995), after careful definition, condemns euthanasia as morally wrong. This is a teaching of highest authority, short of a dogmatic definition, because it is derived rather directly from one of the Commandments. It is one of the hybrid teachings I referred to above. But the very fact that I readily, and almost instinctively, accept this teaching as true should put me on my guard. What hidden, and therefore unexamined, assumptions might I have made? Perhaps I should test out in my imagination various circumstances in which euthanasia might appear desirable. Perhaps the encyclical is not stringent enough and the principle of double effect applied too laxly. Do I really think that the prohibition against murder comprehends euthanasia under all conditions? And, most importantly, what counter-arguments could be mounted against the teaching?

John Stuart Mill, in arguing for the liberty of speech, said that the best guarantee of the truth of an opinion is that it has been openly exposed to free public examination and has withstood all the objections of its opponents. Similarly we do not have the best title for assenting with will and intellect to a truth taught by the Magisterium until we have heard and given full weight to opposing arguments. Interestingly, Mill instances 'the most intolerant of churches, the Roman Catholic Church' for its use of the 'devil's advocate' in the canonization procedure. 'The holiest of men, it appears, cannot be admitted to posthumous honours, until all that the devil could say against him is known and weighed.'[18] Or, I would add, the holiest of doctrine. This scepticism could of course be merely an excuse for playing the gadfly; but correctly used it is an expression of full personal autonomy – a quest to conform oneself more closely to the truth. 'Man's dignity then demands that he should act in accordance with a free and conscious choice, personally, inwardly persuaded, and not by either blind impulse from within or coercion from without.'[19]

By the same token one cannot be confident that a teaching of the Church is not binding without examining with an open mind everything which may be said in its support. What is sauce for Mill's goose is also sauce for his gander.

The Service of Dissent

Dissent is also potentially of service to the Church as a whole. I wrote above of the changes in doctrines such as usury or freedom of religious conscience. Before we puff and splutter at the unchristian ways of the medieval Church it is right to remember how much it was a child of its time then, as it is today. For example, slavery was seen by Aristotle as part of the natural order and, given that it was permitted under the Mosaic law and that St Paul appeared to tolerate it, and given that it was a widespread and generally accepted system of economic importance, it was not surprising that 'This estimate of slavery continued to prevail till it became fixed in the systematized ethical teaching of the schools; and so it remained without any conspicuous modification till towards the end of the eighteenth century.'[20] In other words, throughout eighteen centuries, no one had really stopped to think about it – or, when they did, had not been able to slough off the unconscious influences which prevented them from seeing what to us is as plain as a pikestaff.

It may seem strange to those with short memories that up to the reform of the liturgy consequent on the Council we prayed every Good Friday that God 'who deniest not thy mercy even to the perfidious Jews' should have their blindness of heart relieved.[21] Not that the 'perfidious' Jews ever felt insulted by this because they were forbidden, with a number of other civil disabilities, from appearing in public during Easter Week by the Fourth Lateran Council (1215). Perhaps the relevant decrees are still in force. The general but not universal view that the Jews as members of the people who killed God deserved pretty much everything they got was not formally repudiated until the decree of Vatican II on non-Christian religions. Anti-Semitism tends to be strong in Catholic countries; witness for example France and the Dreyfus Affair, or Poland and its recent apology for its anti-Semitic activities in World War II. Whatever the rights or wrongs of how Pius XII dealt with German anti-Semitism there can be no doubt that European anti-Semitism drew strength over the ages from the ambivalent (and I am being kind) attitude of the Magisterium.[22]

Because the change has been so gradual one has to read a complete account like that given by John T. Noonan[23] to realize the extent of the changes in the Magisterium's attitude towards the use of sexuality, from a deep and unavoidable connection with sin to the rich personalist teaching of *Gaudium et Spes*, which rejoices in sexual love as an expression of the bond of marriage. There is no doubt that if the doctrine of *Gaudium et Spes* had been proposed in former centuries it would have been roundly condemned, on the authority of Augustine, Aquinas and the general teaching of the Magisterium. A meditation given to English seminarians in the later seventeenth century read:

> For the manner of thy begetting is so foule that the name, nay the lightest thought of it, defileth the purest minde, so that our B. Sauiour refused none of our miseries but onely that; and the matter so horrid, so foule, that all other dung is pleasant and greatfull in respect of it; nay we dare not in discourse giue it a name, for our owne shame and others offence . . .[24]

A well-known textbook of moral theology carried, up to 1923, the description of intercourse as *res in se foeda*, a thing filthy in itself; the parts of the body were commonly categorized in moral theologies into the decent, the less decent and the indecent (*partes inhonestae*). You can work out which.[25] This attitude continues, perhaps unconsciously, in lay devotion. A popular Catholic hymn contains the line 'The one spotless womb wherein Jesus was laid'. We sing it without reflecting on the implication that ordinary wombs are spotted by childbearing. A similar expression occurs in the Roman Missal. The suspicion that anything to do with sexual pleasure is somehow shameful is not confined to ecclesiastics but it seems likely that this deep-laid attitude inhibited the growing clarity of the Magisterium's vision.

The ordinary moral teaching of the Magisterium, though given by the delegated authority of Christ, is, as I have noted, subject to the imperfections and limitations of the human condition. Despite Father Davis's claim in his 1934 preface that the excellent work of his predecessors over three centuries has left him no room for originality, moral teaching must continually develop and modify against the test of new circumstances and new understandings.

There is a constant need to review with a critical and reforming eye the influence of great – but not necessarily correct – authorities, of prejudices and inappropriate attitudes, of erroneous science, of custom, inadvertence and convenience. At any one time all that it can do, and this is a very great deal, is to teach the Church's current understanding – necessarily provisional and continually open to the possibility of development or change. She, the whole community from the Pope to the humblest pew-fodder, feels her way through the shadows trying to discern more and more clearly the distinctive features of Christ – she is a pilgrim in transient mode, wearing for now this age's fashion.[26] This task of discovering and refining the truth goes beyond the realm of personal decision; while it may be the function of the Magisterium to articulate teachings it is the function of the whole community to look out and speak up. Anti-Semitism and slavery are just two examples where the impetus for change came primarily from outside the Church; but an active and thoughtful laity could well have been the instruments for earlier reform. From St Paul squaring up to St Peter over the circumcision of Gentile converts[27] until the present, dissent has been an instrument of prophecy and witness. It performs the function outlined by John Stuart Mill of testing the spirits to see if they be of God.[28]

Cardinal Newman, as is well known, regarded the general and shared faith of the laity not only as a desirable but as an essential adjunct to the teaching of the Magisterium; it was an integral part of the Church's expression of her tradition and belief: '... because the body of the faithful is one of the witnesses to the fact of the tradition of revealed doctrine, and because their *consensus* through Christendom is the voice of the Infallible Church'. He notes that the tradition of the Church was handed down to the whole community and that without denying the authority of the Magisterium all the available channels should be treated with respect.[29] In the Dogmatic Constitution on the Church, *Lumen Gentium*, 37, the duty and not merely the right of the laity to make known their opinion on matters concerned with the good of the Church is affirmed.[30]

A Look at Dissent in Action

In Chapter 1 I recorded the view that the Church's teaching on artificial contraception was a trigger event, and that much of the Church's decline can be traced from this. While it is an outstanding example, it remains no more than an example. Its prominence can only too easily cloud the other much deeper issues I have been discussing. So relegating my view of the question to the Appendix will, I hope, avoid distraction from more fundamentally important questions. It will also save those who are heartily sick of the issue, or who regard it as trivial and irrelevant, from being presented with it here.

Summary

Vatican II emphasizes the sovereignty of conscience, but in more than one place it stipulates that it must be formed in accordance with the Church's moral teaching. This apparent incompatibility is best approached by distinguishing infallible teaching from fallible teaching. Ideally, a fallible moral teaching should be validated through our own judgement, but we must prefer the Church's teaching authority when we have good reason to think that it is the best source of the truth.

It would be a great advance if the Magisterium were able to admit more openly that its current moral understanding will, as it has in the past, develop and sometimes change. Other than in infallible matters it can never be more than the best view available at the time. It is well established, but needs to be emphasized, that individual dissent may be justified since the formed judgement of conscience always takes precedence. Open discussion, which could have prevented unfortunate episodes in the past, should be seen as a service rather than disloyalty. Not only can the Magisterium get a fuller picture of what the Church as a community actually believes, but listening and responding to different approaches is also an important means through which moral teaching can be modified or confirmed. The laity need to play a part in this because, as Pius XII pointed out, 'In decisive battles the happiest initiatives often come from the frontline.'[31]

Notes to Chapter 5

1. *www.uiah.fi/bookshop/isea_proc/spacescapes/artcyb/05.html.*
2. *Gaudium et Spes* 17 and 50.
3. *Dignitatis Humanae* 3.
4. *Dignitatis Humanae* 14.
5. I have avoided mention here of the second category of teachings, those which are described in *Ad Tuendam Fidem* (1998) as 'definitive', because this is not necessary for the points I am making. I understand from Father Avery Dulles' article (*Tablet*, 25 July 1998) that it is not clear what this category comprehends, nor its exact status with regard to infallibility, nor the precise meaning of 'definitive'. To the layman the whole thing sounds like a dog's breakfast, but I appreciate that it is a serious matter for those whose office requires them to make the Profession. No doubt the theologians and the Congregation for the Doctrine of the Faith will sort it out one of these decades.
6. Hans Küng, 'Waiting for Vatican III', *Tablet* (16 December 1995).
7. CDF (28 October 1995).
8. *Gaudium et Spes* 27.
9. 'Magisterium', *Encyclopedia of Theology* (Burns & Oates).
10. *Tablet* (20 January 2001).
11. *Syllabus of Errors* (1864). Other documents denying religious freedom are *Letter to the Bishop of Troyes,* by Pope Pius VII (1814), *Mirari Vos,* by Pope Gregory XVI (15 August 1832), *Quanta Cura,* by Pope Pius IX (8 December 1864), *Libertas,* by Pope Leo XIII (20 June 1888). Note also the change in the Concordat with Spain in the light of Vatican II's 'new' teaching on the subject.
12. I am indebted to my historian son, Guy, for the coinage of 'chronocentric' which accurately describes a universal tendency. And we might remember Emerson's remark: 'A foolish consis-

tency is the hobgoblin of little minds, adored by little statesmen, philosophers and divines' (*Self-Reliance*).

13. From John L. Allen Jr's report in the *National Catholic Reporter* (19 April 2002).

14. 'The Authority of the Church's Moral Teaching', *Clergy Review* (September 1967).

15. Phrasing taken from the third category in *Ad Tuendam Fidem*.

16. The position of office holders in the Church, who are obliged to subscribe to *Ad Tuendam fidem*, differs from that of the lay Catholic. It could be argued that acceptance of non-infallible teachings is a condition of holding office, and the only alternative would be to resign. Fortunately tact seems to prevent this issue arising with frequency

17. *The Documents of Vatican II*, ed. Walter M. Abbott (Chapman, 1966).

18. J. S. Mill, *On Liberty* 1 (1859).

19. *Gaudium et Spes* 17.

20. 'Slavery', *Catholic Encyclopedia* (1913).

21. Roman missal.

22. The issue is discussed at length by Garry Wills, *Papal Sin*.

23. *Contraception* (Harvard University Press, 1965).

24. English College of Lisbon (1663). Quoted in Philip Sheldrake, 'Spirituality and Sexuality', in *Embracing Sexuality*, ed. Joseph A. Selling (Ashgate, 2001). This is the less offensive of the two quotes given.

25. Taken from E. C. Messenger, *Two in One Flesh*, Part 1 (Sands & Co., 1948). The moral theologian was P. Noldin, *Theol. Moralis*, and the phrase was excised from later editions. Messenger also recalls the dictum of an old Latin writer though he cannot recall the source: *Inter urinas et faeces nascimur omnes*. Following Gibbon I leave this in the decent obscurity of a learned language.

26. *Lumen Gentium* 48.

27. Gal. 2.11.

28. 1 John 4.1.

29. John Henry Newman, 'On Consulting the Faithful in Matters

of Doctrine', *The Rambler* (July 1859), repr. in John Henry Newman, *Conscience, Consensus and the Development of Doctrine: Revolutionary Texts by John Henry Cardinal Newman*, ed. James Gaffney (Image/Doubleday, 1992), pp. 392–428.

30. The Constitution asks that this should be done through the agencies set up for this purpose. But effective agencies for dissent do not appear to exist. I refer to some problems in communication in the Church in Chapters 7 and 8.

31. Allocution, *De Quelle Consolation* (1951).

CHAPTER 6

THE PROCESS OF CONSCIENCE FORMATION

In essence the formation of conscience means no more, and no less, than taking appropriate care that we make the right moral decision. This is the responsibility that the exercise of our autonomy requires. And almost every decision we make has at least some moral content in that it has a bearing on the proper love we have either for ourselves or for our neighbour. In this respect a morality based on law makes fewer demands than morality based on love – because love gets in everywhere.

Fortunately, however, this does not mean that our daily activities are punctuated by little pauses in which to form our consciences. If, as I outlined in Chapter 4, we have committed ourselves to love of God and neighbour, developed in our holiness and our virtues generally, then good moral decisions in most instances are made without deliberate thought. The conscience has, if you wish, been pre-formed.

> A skilled and experienced car driver makes many good driving decisions in the course of a single minute. His response is an instinctive reaction arising out of his developed skills. He only needs to take deliberate thought when he meets an unfamiliar situation. A poor or inexperienced driver may be tentative or over-confident. He will make a much larger proportion of bad decisions.

However, it is prudent to check one's instinctive moral decisions; it is only too easy for them to deteriorate – as may happen with driving skills. The regular examination of conscience to review what one has done right as well as what one has done wrong (described in Chapter 4) is helpful here. And note the comments on 'little by little' below.

It is only when we are uncertain about what we should do for the best, and particularly when we come up against a conflict of values, that we have to deliberate. The care with which the decision is made will be proportionate to the gravity of the values involved.

> One of your children has a medical condition which can be best helped by treatment which is only available privately and not through the State system. But the cost will be at the expense of other members of the family who may suffer educationally as a result.
>
> This sort of decision may need many factors to be carefully weighed. And even when the decision is made you will not know whether it has been made for the best.

The Holistic Conscience

This fashionable phrase is shorthand for the idea that since decisions of conscience are a response of the whole person to love, so the making of the decision – or the formation of conscience – involves the whole person. The idea of conscience being a judicial activity in which the proposed action is judged against the requirements of the law has its place in the textbook, or when a judgement is being made about the actions of someone else, but it is not what happens in real life.

The complete human being faces decisions with a multitude of elements – feelings, assumptions, habits of mind, perceptions, social pressures, teachings of parents and Church – in addition to reason. That sounds as if moral decisions are very subjective, very much more derived from the context in which they take place than from objective right or wrong. Yet reason is not just another item on the list. If I may continue my driving analogy, what we do on the road does depend on conditions and also on the performance and characteristics of the car, yet the final control lies in the decisions we make about steering, accelerator and brake. So reason plays the crucial part in conscience formation, judging all the other human elements against right and wrong. This process will become clearer as we see it in action.

Preparation

I have indicated that the groundwork for good conscience formation lies in the kind of person we have become through our commitment to the good, the practice of virtue and the quality of previous decisions. But at the time new decisions have to be made the die in that respect is cast. I am in no way qualified to give spiritual advice so I can only report on my personal experience here. I have found that praying about a decision of conscience is immensely helpful – although not necessarily comfortable, since the result is sometimes an answer I would rather have avoided.

At the (apparently) human level it is difficult to avoid unwelcome issues or facing up to internal weaknesses. Excuses seem pointless when both the Holy Spirit and I know their worthlessness. In contrast, I find that prayer releases a creativity in me: I am able to see matters not only with more clarity but also in a more creative way. Ideas, new insights and original solutions often occur. I do not mean that in some magical way inspiration comes from on high; I still have to work through my normal mental processes. But in some fashion that I do not understand I find it possible at the same time to entrust my thinking to the Holy Spirit in a confidence born of experience that I will find a way through.

At the very least it is hard to pray sincerely and form one's conscience insincerely.

The Methods of the Counsellor

People who come for marriage counselling are always faced by decisions of conscience, although they often do not recognize them as such. Generally the problems are dramatic because on their solution depends the preservation of a marriage and it therefore affects the lives of a number of people, and because it is usually only desperation, after a long period of difficulties, which brings them to the counselling room. Feelings are running high, and they are mostly negative. The only point of light is that somewhere, somehow, there is at least the vestige of a hope that all may eventually be well.

I have come to believe that the point of light is the Holy Spirit. And it is that ultimate orientation towards the good and the loving which provides the positive motivating force. In Chapter 4 I spoke of the buoyancy of a cork in a bucket of water. It would naturally spring to the surface were it not for the obstructions which keep it down. The work of the counsellor is not to inspire or persuade, it is to help the client to clear away the obstructions so that his natural (I would rather say, supernatural) buoyancy can carry him upwards.

The counsellor, then, is not an agent but a catalyst. Although, in the natural way of things, he cannot help the effect of his personal influence, his objective is to work from inside the client. He does not do the work but he aims to provide the condition and the methodology through which the client's work will be done. And that work is the formation of conscience.

Counsellors are often asked how often they achieve 'success' in their work. Apart from the obvious difficulty of checking on the long-term effects, what would count as success will vary from case to case. In the end I concluded that I had achieved some, unquantified, degree of success if a client was, at the end of the process, able to make a freer – that is, more human – decision. Some at least of the negatives holding the cork down should have been removed, enabling the cork to rise further towards its own true level. Conscience, for all its imperatives, is not infallible but its good formation should enable a freer, more autonomous and thus more human decision to be made.

So, in this chapter, I will use the model of counselling to look at conscience formation. Because of the complexity and the depth of counselling problems, the process may take a far longer period of time than most of us need, or indeed have available, for our moral decisions. Yet the elements detailed here do appear at some level in ordinary decisions of conscience, although the importance they have may vary from situation to situation.

Feelings and Emotions

Feelings are a reaction at the emotional level to our experiences of life. They may be fleeting and changeable or they may be characteristic of how we as an individual react. This may be a reflection of past experiences, including the sort of person we have trained ourselves to be through the practice of virtue. Sometimes they are long-term because they are a response to a long-term situation. Typically our immediate reaction to and judgement of a situation are made through feelings, and they are a strong motivator to action. It is nearly impossible to carry out a rational decision which is strongly at variance with our feelings. And in fact feelings can have a considerable influence on the conclusions to which our reasoning comes. So they are extremely powerful and, although we may be rightly confident that they steer us in the direction of the good, they are pre-moral. That is, they play a part in the moral equation but are not, taken in themselves, either right or wrong.

Faced by a dilemma with emotional content one is likely to have a confused mixture of feelings.

> You have discovered an employee of yours behaving dishonestly. You need to consider what to do. Your feelings are a jumble but they include: resentment at being let down by a trusted colleague; the liking you have always had for this person; fear that someone might blame you for trusting him; worry that his dishonesties may have occurred before; a concern for his future welfare; a concern for your customers or shareholders who may have suffered; concern for his family; guilt about whether in some way you have contributed to the offence; worry about whether to inform the legal authorities or deal with the matter yourself.

You could add many other possible items to the list. Without even having to consider your feelings carefully you might be aware that some of them are not perhaps as helpful as others. For instance, your fear that someone might blame you for not spotting the situation earlier might seem to you to be unworthy. But this may become clearer when you face up to all the feelings which you actually have.

Most people have an unfortunate instinct for attempting to censor the feelings they are ashamed to have. This is most easily done by refusing to look at them. Unfortunately this does not lead to them going away. Another strategy is to look at them and, by concentration of the will, try to expunge them. One might as well try, by taking thought, to add one cubit to one's stature.

The way most likely to succeed, which the counselling room confirms, is to articulate all the feelings bad and good, and then admit explicitly that you have them. And that you have a right to have them in the sense that you do not choose your feelings – they come unbidden. They may or may not correspond to reality but they are in themselves a reality because you in reality feel them. This admission of feelings and the right to have them changes their psychological status. Instead of seeing the feelings as somehow being part of you ('because I have selfish feelings I am a selfish person') they become objects outside you, which you happen to have. This frees you to look at your feelings set up, so to speak, in a row in front of you – a row that you can now evaluate. You may then judge, through your reason, that some of the feelings are unhelpful. For instance you might recognize false guilt, or some irrational fear based on a natural vulnerability. You may rank others in some kind of order of importance, and you may accept that one feeling is incompatible with another and that you may have to live with this incompatibility.

You do not then attempt to expunge the unhelpful feelings. You are, you remember, entitled to have them. But by some strange alchemy they wilt under the light of your calm judgement. Unhelpful feelings are like mushrooms: they flourish in the dark but when exposed to the light they die quickly. But waste no time watching them die – it only aggravates them; leave them to get on with it and at some future time you will realize that they are simply no longer there.

False guilt (about which I wrote in Chapter 4 under the virtue of self-esteem) provides a common example of unhelpful feelings. A person may well feel guilty about some incident for which their reason tells them they were not responsible. Its presence may even cause a kind of psychological paralysis. By accepting that they have this feeling of guilt, looking at it objectively and consciously denying responsibility, and then getting on with the next task without adverting to it again, is the best way to allow the feeling to wither on the vine.

Those of a psychoanalytic turn of mind may suggest that another way of drawing the sting from feelings is to come to understand the unconscious motivations bred from past experience which have caused them. By giving a plausible story (in the nature of things difficult to prove) which explains current feelings, one may be relieved from their pressure. It does seem rather demanding to require psychoanalysis in order to form the conscience, though I cannot deny that many who have undergone this report valuable insights and beneficial changes. At a humbler level I have found that clients are sometimes freed by being able to link, say, a habitual way of thinking to their upbringing, or recognizing the part that a particular incident, say, the death of a parent, may have played. But I am wary lest they conclude that with such a history they cannot be expected to change. It is better to put the past back where it belongs – behind them; and concentrate on the present and what to do about it.

I am writing here of the normal range of inappropriate feelings which we all have from time to time. But if the feelings are deep-set and really inhibit constructive and progressive action it may well be that professional help is needed. Professional counselling services are widely available and one should always consider the possibility of psychotherapy. I lean towards cognitive therapy, which is consonant with the ideas I have given above.

It is often assumed that while women are relatively at home in dealing with and articulating feelings, men find this difficult and counter to their cultural conditioning. This needs qualification. While men are often unused to talking about their feelings, they seize the opportunity eagerly when it is offered – perhaps because it is so rare. Arguably our culture imposes a burden on men by inhibiting their opportunities to come to terms with their feelings through expressing them.

> I was brought up in a family in which strong feelings were thought rather bad form. However, they could be quickly exorcised by a joke. It was not until I was married to someone in touch with her feelings that I first truly learnt about the emotional life – but the scars remain.

So feelings are the first element which come under consideration. It is important to articulate the feelings, and accept that you have them. It is then possible to judge how and to what extent they are appropriate and helpful.

Assumptions

We all come to judgements with a bundle of assumptions which we have learned from past experience. It is an assumption that someone who has been dishonest once will be dishonest again; it is an assumption that someone who has cheated on their spouse is untrustworthy in politics. It is an assumption that shareholders should always be considered before employees; it is an assumption that employees should be considered before shareholders. It is an assumption that men are naturally promiscuous; it is an assumption that women are naturally faithful. It is an assumption that men are unable to recognize and express their feelings. It is an assumption that a rebellious teenager is acting from malice, or, for that matter, that his upbringing or environment relieve him of all responsibility.

Some of our assumptions may have been learnt from our parents or peer groups, others may be a reasonable deduction from experience, others may be the result of prejudice. Stereotyping is a common form of assumption – students are unreliable, Asians are hard workers, men are emotionally illiterate, and so on.

We cannot operate without assumptions because we simply do not have time to think out every situation we encounter from scratch. We all have a series of pre-packed judgements in our mind, and we reach up into our mental shelves to bring down the packages which we think apply to the situation in hand. And to a large extent our assumptions define us: 'our prejudices far more than our judgements constitute our historical existence'.[1] But it is possible to review our assumptions and test them for truth, as well as their applicability to a specific situation. It was once said that a young man who is not a socialist needs his heart examined while an old man who is a socialist needs his head examined. So life can change assumptions. Similarly our practice of the habits of virtue can change our assumptions and make them more reliable. But at the point of moral decision we should be clear about the assumptions we are making, just as we need to be clear about our feelings. At the very least we can then judge with our reason what weight they should be given in our deliberation.

Knowledge

Just as we can be trapped by unhelpful emotions or assumptions so we can be trapped by simple lack of knowledge. For instance someone considering abortion as a solution to a problem needs to know all the realistic alternatives before they can make a free decision. Similarly someone contemplating divorce or separation needs to have some idea of the likely consequences both for themselves and for the children involved. Or, to refer to the example above about the medical needs of a child, there may be other ways of obtaining medical help which will not affect the remaining children. The moral teaching and understanding of the Church is another aspect of knowledge which may be necessary. I deal with this further below.

Naturally some people have a better background knowledge than others, or better access to sources of information. But part of the process of conscience formation may often be to ask oneself what one needs to know in order to make the best decision, and then to see if one can obtain it.

Habitual Ways of Thinking

Closely related to assumptions are habitual ways of thinking and judging. Many of these are particular to us. If I am inclined to favour the underdog, for example, I could find myself being unjust to another party. In the example of the dishonest employee I gave above I have to weigh what is due to the owners of the business against what is due to my errant colleague. Without being aware that my attitude is habitual, and therefore needs testing, I risk being guilty of injustice. If, in the interests of avoiding sentimentality, I am habitually careful to judge situations through a rather rigid analysis I may not spot a human dimension to a moral dilemma which could be an important factor. The individual who consistently opposes establishment authority embraces one group of habitual ways of thinking; someone who consistently conforms to establishment authority embraces another. Where do you stand between the extremes of pessimism and optimism? It can make a considerable difference to how we judge circumstances, but not to the circumstances themselves. It is only when we are aware of the biases in our habits of thinking that we can challenge them through our rational judgement.

By Their Fruits

In looking at attitudes and habitual ways of thinking, it is important to carry out a reality check by reviewing behaviour. You may hold that children are more important than animals, but which charities do you actually support? You may think that the young have good ideas, but how often do you allow their opinions to influence you? You may believe in delegation but how do your delegates see this quality in you? You may hold that your spouse is the most important person for you, but does the conduct of your life reflect that? Our capacity for self-deceit seems bottomless. Fortunately we have the evangelical counsel to judge by the fruits. Painful, but revealing.

Back in the counselling room the marriage counsellor will be sensitive to apparent patterns of behaviour, because these can throw light on habitual ways of thinking and acting. For example a counsellor might say: 'I notice that most often when you have a big row with your wife it's when you've just come back from a business trip. Is that just coincidence or is it connected with the problem?' Of course it may be either, but quite often the client recognizes a pattern and gets closer to understanding the heart of the difficulty. Similarly an inconsistency can sometimes be revealing: 'You tell me that you've been working very hard for your exams but this evening you said that your father told you off for being out too much in the evenings. I don't see how that fits together, or have I misunderstood something?' Patterns and inconsistencies are both ways of testing what is really happening by observing behaviour. An individual who is aware of the possibility is able to use these methods to face up to differences between what they think they believe and what they actually do.

Common Habits of Human Nature

Alongside the habits of thinking which are particular to us are the habits which appear to be generally common to human nature. They are often difficult to spot because they are so ingrained that considerable insight is needed to identify them. Here are just a few examples.

Little by Little

The human system operates by reacting to changes. But if the changes are small enough they can escape notice, even though they are cumulative. We sometimes fail to notice how our car has got out of tune until the annual service puts it right. Similarly, bad habits – for instance a carelessness about truth – can grow to a serious degree without our realizing it. A Christian, despite his orientation to eternal values, can forget the old saying: 'There are no pockets in a shroud.' It is a long way from a humble fisherman in Galilee to the material comforts of modern suburban life. But it does not seem a long way when it is taken in small steps.

> A friend of mine told me how upset he had been when a valuable table lamp was accidentally broken. Only later did he realize that his annoyance was a measure of how much importance he had come to put on material objects, and how inconsistent this was with his Christian vocation. That story made me think about myself, too.

Judgement by Externals

It is plausible that our well-documented tendency to make swift decisions on the basis of little evidence is evolutionary in origin. The imperative to avoid danger or obtain food favoured those who made snap judgements. So we commonly see tall people as more important than short, or people wearing glasses as more intelligent than those who do not, or attractive people as more virtuous than the ill-favoured. There are many other unconscious assumptions which have been well tested by psychology.

> It was made clear to me during my career in financial services that my beard, small and neat though it was, put me at a disadvantage in the promotion stakes. I did not fit the orthodox image. Perhaps I would have been Governor of the Bank of England by now if I had complied!

Prejudice against foreigners, in particular those of a different colour or with an unfamiliar culture, is widespread – even amongst those who are sincerely convinced that they are liberals. It may perhaps be an overhang from some primitive instinct that strangers are dangerous and should be treated as enemies. These and similar factors can affect moral judgement if they are allowed to.[2]

Selective Memory

Many people are convinced that they pay little attention to first impressions, yet all the studies show that not only is this common but that we pay more attention to happenings which confirm the impression and ignore those which might alter it – thus tending to reinforce the initial response. This in itself can lead to unfair judgements but it also indicates how good people are at remembering just what suits them – and being quite sincere about it – and, as a general point, how good we are at altering our picture of reality to make it conform with our view.

> One engaged couple whom I counselled could give, in front of each other, a very different account of an incident which had occurred that same day. Their selective memories and individual interpretations led them, in all sincerity, to different and incompatible recollection.

Social Pressure

If we are inclined to doubt that social pressure affects our moral choice you may like to consider the herd instinct. When I looked at the virtue of social independence, in Chapter 4, I discussed the strong influence wielded by the group in which we belong. Evolutionists suggest that the herd instinct developed as a primitive safety ploy. Generally our remote ancestors had a better chance of survival if they stayed with the group instead of going it alone, only to be picked off by a predator. So we may have inherited the genes of those conformist ancestors, since the others rarely lived to breed. And society needs a good deal of conformity in order to survive; consequently it applies many overt and covert pressures to discourage those who think for themselves and act accordingly. Yet the Christian in virtue of his vocation must always be ready to set his own standards. That pressure to conform remains with us, and – on the whole – the conformist still has the quiet life, while non-conformity may well prove uncomfortable. It is hard to understand the voluntary collusion of the Germans with anti-Jewish policies during the 1930s without acknowledging a strong element of voluntary acceptance of group values.

It might be an interesting exercise to list the values of our society and then consider whether those to which we in fact subscribe are good or not. Repeat the exercise using the society of Catholics-like-us; and again, using the values of the Magisterium. In each case, of course, the values should be identified by how people (including ourselves) actually behave, not what they proclaim. If you are unable to spot points at which you differ from any of these groups then you must either be living at a very fortunate point in time or completely ruled by the values of others. The briefest survey of history shows a multitude of values which were taken for granted by right-thinking people in the past which today their counterparts would be the first to condemn. It would be naive to suppose that the same situation does not obtain today.

As I write there is much in the media condemning, almost ritually, the Palestinian suicide bombers who kill and maim innocent civilians. Yet fifty years earlier very similar people supported the Allied mass bombing of civilian populations in World War II. The moral status of attacking civilians has not changed, but the perspective has.

So it would be prudent to accept that we are all, often unconsciously, inclined to take our standards and assumptions from the group to which we belong; and to incorporate this insight into conscience formation.

The Church as Teacher

I have discussed at some length in Chapter 5 the role of the Church's teaching authority so at this stage I need do little more than reinforce its importance. The Church has authority from God to teach; and we must respond accordingly. Even looking at it in mere human terms it is an authority which has contemplated human nature and the ends it was created for over two millennia. The extent of human wisdom it has accumulated is immense. In addition, it sees this in the light of the deeper dimension of Revelation. Part Three of the *Catechism of the Catholic Church* is a major section devoted to Life in the Spirit and the Ten Commandments. It is invaluable as a means of seeing the principles of the moral life clearly and the inferences that may be drawn from them for decisions of conscience. Moral teaching is often to be found in pastoral letters and the like (the Bishops of England and Wales, for instance, summarize the social teaching of the Church as they see it applying to the issues of a general election). It is hard to see how anyone can claim to have formed his conscience properly without being open to these teachings and attempting to understand just how they conform to reason. There may be some circumstances in which they do not apply or do not provide clear guidance, and there may be a few instances where, after serious consideration, one is not able to agree. And here the Church herself is the first champion of not only the freedom but also the obligation to follow the truth as one understands it. Once again one cannot avoid making judgements of reason.

Perception

Perceptions are neither feelings nor assumptions; they are a clear recognition that something is or is not so. They are not infallible – since others may with equal sincerity hold an incompatible perception – but they are subjectively certain and therefore command the conscience.

Our grasp of the natural law is the result of perception: through it we recognize the foundational principle that good ought to be done, and its broad demands, as enshrined in the Commandments and the ultimate call to love God and neighbour. None of these can be incontrovertibly demonstrated – they can only be perceived.

Psychologists do not fully understand perceptions, any more than theologians, but at the personal level the experience is of seeing a truth directly, somehow transcending all the arguments and questions that might otherwise cloud the issue. Jesus, we may imagine, was responding to perception when he saw, and taught, that human needs took precedence over the, very important and God-given, law of the Sabbath.

> Franz Jägerstätter, Martyr, repudiated Nazi ideology and refused to join the German army, despite the persuasion of his priest and bishop. His perception of evil could not be expunged by arguments of conventional morality or the authority of his spiritual superiors. He was beheaded in 1943.

Similarly there are those who perceive that the prohibition of the use of condoms in the presence of an Aids pandemic in Africa is plainly wrong, others may not. And there are those who perceive that using contraception in casual sex lessens rather than compounds the offence – and those who don't.

Accurate perception has a quality of 'out of the mouths of babes and sucklings' about it. It appears to require an almost naive clarity of vision, and fundamental orientation towards the true good. That does not mean that a perception should not undergo the judgement of reason. One may imagine that Jägerstätter thought long about his bishop's representations before confirming his original perception.

> The late Donald Nicholl, who was a student in Germany during the rise of Nazism, was surprised to see how many good Catholics found justifiable reasons to join the Nazi Party. But one of his friends, somewhat less intellectual than the rest, refused. When asked why he simply said: 'I cannot believe that a movement which encourages its members to hate other human beings is right, no matter what the other arguments may be.'

Approaches to Decision Making

There are a number of ways – tools if you like – which have been found helpful in sorting out the tangles which inhibit decision making.

Applying the Golden Rule

Apply the Golden Rule – do unto others as you would have them do unto you – to all the people immediately affected by the decision. In Chapter 4 I discussed the virtue of empathy – the habit of seeing the world from the perspective of others. Only through this can we truly love our neighbours as ourselves. At the time of forming the conscience this habit really comes into its own. Moral situations can take on quite a different colour when seen in this way. How does it feel to be taken for granted in a domestic situation? How does it feel to be forced out of business by a tough competitor? How does it feel to be lied to by someone you trusted? How does it feel to have your reputation sullied by gossip? How does it feel to be a child who thinks his parents disapprove of him? How does it feel to find sexual relations with the opposite sex revolting but to be strongly drawn to one's own? How does it feel to experience a strong call to the priesthood but to be excluded because of gender? How does it feel to return to your car and find a bad scrape on the wing, but no one ready to own up? It is a strange quirk of human nature that we often apply different standards to ourselves from the ones we apply to other people whose actions affect us. But it is hard to maintain a different standard when we have really seen the situation as the other person sees it.

Different Frames of Reference

Seeing a situation from another's point of view is an example of change in frame of reference. Following King David's seduction of Bathsheba Nathan asked him how should a man be punished if he had stolen a poor man's only ewe lamb. David said: 'The man who hath done this deserves to die.' Nathan replied: 'You are the man.' And David saw the truth and said: 'I have sinned against the Lord.'³ But there are other kinds of frame of reference. For example, if you are asked to agree to your widowed mother-in-law living with you permanently, your frame might be the solidarity of extended family support, or the frame of your first obligation being to the quality of your own marriage, or the frame of the advantage or disadvantage to your children. Each frame may give you a different answer, and you may have to decide between them. But it is important to look beyond the frame of reference which initially comes to mind, and explore other ways of looking at the situation.

Examining Consequences

A Christian cannot base his moral choices solely on a weighing up of consequences – based, for example, on the greatest happiness of the greatest number. The best of ends cannot justify an evil means. But in the ordinary way a careful consideration of the short- and long-term consequences of alternative choices will be needed. Among these, but not always considered, is the question of principle. Were one, for instance, to be considering hastening directly the death of an elderly relative in pain (euthanasia), what would be the effect of accepting for oneself (and by the same token for others) the breach of the principle of the sacredness of human life? It is only necessary to reflect on the resulting effects (so far) of the legalization of abortion, which was, at least initially, advocated by well-meaning and compassionate people, to see how long and how tortuous a path entered by one step can become.[4]

Consulting Others

Other people may be a source of knowledge or information as I described above, but I have in mind here the help we can often obtain in sorting out the tangle. Discrimination is required. Some people may give persuasive advice based on little more than their opinions, which are potentially as contaminated as your own. We may have a strong need to have our decisions made for us; somehow we feel we can shuffle off responsibility through taking another's view – or even several others, in the hope of finding a majority. But if you are fortunate enough to have a friend or a back-up group who can genuinely help you to see the wood from the trees without interfering with your decision, then you are lucky indeed. It will not always be a professional 'helper', sometimes it will be a spouse or a best friend.

Double Effect

The principle of double effect is often invoked in moral discussion in a wide range of fields. It becomes relevant when a contemplated action will have two effects, one bad and one good. For example, to report a friend to the police for criminal activities would have the effect of stopping his nefarious behaviour, but his innocent wife and children would suffer. The principle requires four questions to be answered in the positive. Is the action in itself at least morally neutral? Is the good it brings about proportionate to the evil done? Is the evil done only an indirect consequence of the action? Is the evil done not intended? In the example I have given, it is quite possible that the action would be justified, despite the evil effect. But in the case, say, of choosing an abortion in order to avoid an unwanted pregnancy, the act of abortion itself is wrong, and the principle cannot be invoked.

Double effect plays a large part in medical ethics: for instance, is the cloning of human embryos justified for the sake of obtaining biological material which may cure intransigent serious diseases? Well before the moral dilemmas raised by the latest scientific discoveries Father Gerald Kelly listed sixty norms in his *Medico-Moral Problems*, many of which hinge on the application of this principle.[5]

Joint Conscience

Some decisions have to be taken jointly. The obvious examples are a husband and wife making a decision about their children or their life together. But there are many other situations in which shared responsibility means that the rights of more than one conscience may be involved. The law-based model inclines towards deciding what is right and holding out against the other if they disagree. The love-based model inclines towards giving an equal respect to the conscience of the other and looking for a compromise which achieves the best balance – without always being entirely satisfactory from either's point of view.

Theoretically at least a compromise between husband and wife who are united in their fundamental objectives will work best. There is good evidence that men have a more justice-oriented conscience and women a more relationship-based conscience.[6] The compromise may then give an objectively better solution than either on their own.

Arriving at Decisions

The ultimate objective of forming one's conscience is to discern what love demands in this situation – a love informed by our innate grasp of right and wrong which we know as the natural law. It is potentially a complex process taking into account a whole range of factors but ultimately subordinated to the truth as we can best discover it through reason.

In the counselling process it is quite common for both client and counsellor to spend some time lost in the undergrowth. It is only after a good deal of exploration, and reflection on the outcomes of exploration, that the picture clears, the important issues stand out, and possible solutions present themselves. Rarely are the solutions easy and often a price has to be paid. Frequently compromises are necessary and the best of competing evils has to be chosen. It is much the same with moral decisions. It is usually only in textbooks that the simple answers are to be found; in real life there is ambiguity and uncertainty. But decisions have to be taken if taking no decision is the worst choice of all.

A long-term friend of mine, a senior actuary, told me that he always judged performance by the quality of the decision rather than by the outcome. His view, as an expert in probability, was that actual outcomes had a big admixture of chance for which one could not be held responsible. But one could be held responsible for the quality of the decision itself.

And if we have done our very best to discover through the use of all our faculties and resources, under the judgement of reason, to discern what love requires, that is all God asks for in the formation of conscience.

Introducing Proper Conscience Formation

Introducing conscience formation along these lines would not in itself be difficult. The usual method of using actual or fictional situations in which a moral decision was required would apply, and in a training situation it would only be necessary to familiarize students with the different factors which would need to be considered in order to arrive at the best solution.

Perhaps the biggest problem would be the instructor's natural pull towards inculcating orthodoxy. For example, some instructors might find it hard to cope with someone who continued, after forming their conscience, to believe in moral justification for some issue which the instructor holds to be intrinsically wrong. A similar problem is encountered by marriage counsellors who find it hard not to use their position of (relative) authority to push their own values. One of the criteria used for selecting counsellors is whether they have a capacity for respecting others' decisions even when they believe them to be wrong or mistaken. It follows of course from the basic principles of conscience that the conscientious decisions of others must be respected. This does not prevent either the counsellor or the instructor from bearing witness to their own beliefs. One must distinguish clearly between instructing someone in the Church's teaching on moral questions and instructing someone in how to form an autonomous conscience. The two tasks are quite different.

I once had the experience of being interviewed by a parish priest with a view to providing a counselling service for his parishioners. He told me he would only be happy provided I could assure him that I would give my clients exactly the same teaching as the Pope would, were he sitting in my place. I tried, but failed, to explain that counselling was not about teaching doctrine but helping people to make the best judgements they could. We had no meeting of minds.

In a way, that parish priest is symbolic of how the Church, at least in its second millennium, became – like the secular institutions of the time – a strongly hierarchical institution invoking, in the Church's case, divine authority for exercising her powers of governance and control. Institutions of this nature may accept the theory of autonomy but do not find it easy in practice. For many, the idea that one might actually encourage people to examine official teaching critically and require them to validate it would be a step too far. Yet it is a step no higher than the Church has taken in the past. A delegate at the Fourth Lateran Council (1215) would be amazed to be transported through time to the Church of today. He would see it as having largely abdicated its authority, become soft at the centre, been infected by the gross instincts of the rabble and a traitor to much doctrine. He would hope that this was no more than a nightmare and that he would soon wake up comfortably in his own bed with his sword stained with the blood of heretics at its foot. But what in fact has happened is that the Church has been dragged, often unwillingly, by the forces of social change into more enlightened ways of behaviour. The cracks in the dictatorial approach to authority are already beginning to appear – Vatican II fatally undermined the foundations. Many, and in influential positions, have been anxious to fill in the cracks as quickly as possible, but movements towards freedom may be delayed but are not often stopped. High-quality secular institutions are about fifty years ahead of today's Church in terms of the enlightened use of authority and, in time, as ever, she will catch up.

The choice is stark: either take the formation of the autonomous conscience seriously and teach it, or see more and more of her members opt out – either partially or completely – since they no longer recognize that the Church can or should form their consciences for them. Ironically, the very freedom of the autonomous conscience can lead to the individual being more open to the influence of the Church than can the straitjacket of unarguable commands.

Summary

Most of our moral decisions are taken in the light of the person we have become, but decisions which require careful conscience formation occur from time to time. The formation of conscience is done by the whole person and involves feelings, assumptions, habits of thinking, knowledge and perceptions. But over all reason reigns. The Church's moral teaching is an important element in this consideration but does not invariably prevail.

Arriving at decisions is not always easy although there are principles such as the Golden Rule or double effect which may well help. Not every decision will be satisfactory but we are only asked to do the best we can.

It is important for the Church to teach the true formation of the autonomous conscience and, in doing so, she may open people more readily to the wisdom and relevance of her moral teaching.

Notes to Chapter 6

1. T. R. Kopfensteiner, 'The Theory of the Fundamental Option and Moral Action', in *Christian Ethics*, ed. Bernard Hoose (Continuum, 1998).
2. I have discussed a number of these issues at greater length in *Getting What You Want* (Piatkus, 1994).
3. 2 Sam. 12, *passim*.
4. There is even an unofficial Catholic organization in the USA, with its own website, which not only advocates a woman's 'right

to choose', but provides a winsome liturgy to accompany the choice. Can you imagine a closer neighbour to love than the child in your womb?

5. Clonmore & Reynolds, 1960.
6. See, for instance, Carol Gilligan, *In a Different Voice: Psychological Theory and Women's Development* (Harvard University Press, 1982).

CHAPTER 7

THE CHURCH AND MODERN MANAGEMENT

'... many claim the right to organize the Church as if she were a multinational corporation and thus subject to a purely human form of authority. In reality, the Church as mystery is not "our" but "his" Church: the People of God, the Body of Christ and the Temple of the Holy Spirit.' So wrote the Holy Father to the German Bishops, referring to a tendency noted by the Extraordinary Synod of 1985 of certain lay organizations which 'critically consider the Church a mere institution'.[1]

It would be a strange theology to see the Church as a 'mere institution'; but it would be equally strange not to recognize that it is *also* an institution and therefore obeys the general rules of human behaviour which are common to institutions. In this chapter I want to examine the Church from that point of view.

All institutions have factors which are unique to them – because of their purpose and their origins. The Church is no different and its particular, and very important, characteristics are epitomized in the Pope's remarks above. However, there are many aspects of the operation of the Church which could benefit from being examined as though it were a 'multinational corporation'. Having worked in, written about and provided consultancy services for multinational corporations for over forty years I believe I have a rounded picture of how they have evolved to meet the needs of their members and customers in a quickly changing society. Clearly Christ's Church has some essential differences, and I will look at these in the appropriate place. Of course, where any characteristic of a secular institution is incompatible with the Church's essential nature it must be excluded.

In discussing the understanding and promotion of the autonomy of the individual conscience I have borne in mind that the principles apply, and should apply, throughout the whole structure of the

Church. It cannot just be a liberal addendum at the individual level to an organization which operates on centralist principles. The question is how to preserve the authority of the Church's mission (and the good order required by any organization) while maintaining the autonomy of its members at different levels. But before scratching our heads, it could help to look at organizations which have already faced and solved the problem. Fortunately they abound.

Modern Management Thinking – the Tight–Loose Principle

Changes in management thinking are in essence based on a new understanding of the human relationship to work. The move has been from regarding workers as tools in the process who are only made effective by a system of rewards and punishments to regarding them as responsible, motivated and actively participating in the goals of the organization.[2] This followed work on the nature of motivation which showed that, once the basic needs were satisfied, motivation came from higher needs such as the need to be loved, and for autonomy and self-fulfilment.[3] Businesses which work in this way have a great advantage because they are tapping greater resources. The background to this change was of course the better education of the workforce, whose basic needs in Western society were routinely met, and the changes in the nature of work which required more fully human input. The worker was no longer a robot with a brain, but a human being meeting his personal aspirations through his work.

This required a corresponding change in the nature of leadership, as distinct from management. Management is primarily concerned with running an ongoing process as effectively as possible; leadership requires a clear view of the future of the business, an accurate picture of its strengths and weakness, and a firm grasp of the (often) relatively few essentials which have to be got right. It is a crucial quality and the spirit of the business is set from the top. The leadership vision of what the business is really about and where it is going must be credible to the whole community, and must infuse its members at every level. Influence is the major tool of the leader and has in practice much greater effect on the welfare of the business than the exercise of power as used in the older forms of management. However, the formal power and hierarchy remains intact, and is used where necessary, but only where necessary, to regulate and secure the business; this is called the tight–loose principle. The same general approach is repeated in microcosm throughout the levels of the organization, and within each business unit, large or small. However great the active participation of all levels in the objectives of the business it is leadership from the top which gives direction, inspiration and coordination. The Petrine office of strengthening, feeding, binding and loosing are – by no coincidence – a good description of the service of secular leadership to the organization.

> I wrote in Chapter 4 of parenting as the management of separation. There is a parallel here. Parents are continually looking for appropriate ways to optimize their children's autonomy while never reneging on their responsibility to maintain the fundamental rules of family living.

Good communication is not only a necessary means of achieving this, it is also a characteristic which identifies such a business. Communication travels upwards, downwards and laterally – binding the community together into a cooperative enterprise under the leadership, enabling the business to benefit from its full human resources.

> The late Donald Nicholl reported on a study carried out by the sociologist Professor Revans. In summary, Revans was asked to investigate why a number of hospitals had a very high turnover of student nurses. He discovered that this turnover operated at all levels: it was also high for qualified nurses and for the medical staff. He then looked at a comparison group of hospitals where there was a low turnover of student staff, and found that there was also low turnover in the higher echelons. The only instance of low turnover in the dysfunctional hospitals was in patients. They simply took longer to recover than in the comparison group.

He then investigated what major differences there were between the two groups, and eventually he discovered that it lay in communication. In the dysfunctional hospitals communication was almost entirely downwards. Information was relayed down the hierarchy but there was little or no traffic in the opposite direction, and the patients were treated as idiots. Nor was there much horizontal communication; in fact relationships were generally poor and marked by antagonism. The level of professional cooperation was low. Conversely the comparison group had continual communication upwards from the patients through to the consultants as well as downwards; horizontal communication was excellent and the various elements worked together at the common task of curing the sick. Revans's opinion was that a change in the situation could only be brought about from the top.[4]

Operating in this way requires certain attitudes and beliefs on the part of management, and these must be sincere – execution, not words, is required. Some managers, through temperament or as a result of past experience, find this very difficult. And it can be hard to develop this approach in a business which has always used traditional authoritarian methods. Workforces in such businesses have been habituated to accepting instructions and will not necessarily welcome change – their autonomy has been, so to speak, knocked out of them and replaced by latent antagonism. Moreover, authoritarian businesses tend to be self-reproducing. That is, they attract those who subscribe to the culture and are managed by people who have succeeded by conforming to it. Such cultures are hard to change. There may even be a fall in the effectiveness of the business until the new culture is bedded in and generally accepted. Consequently many modern businesses, despite their claims, do not practise this new approach or do so only in part. Perhaps the worst of both worlds occurs when a business subscribes overtly to the new principles of management but covertly retains just the same totalitarianism as before – though using a different vocabulary, thus making it harder to challenge.

The Church through the Management Consultant's Eyes

When we look at the characteristics of the Church we see that many of these are in line with these good modern principles – and in some respects well ahead of them. A secular observer looking through business eyes at how the modern Church accords with this new understanding, and reviewing it in terms of its own statements about itself, might make the following summary:

It is a community by its very nature, with a divine founder and protector. Its members are joined through baptism and receive a common call to live up to its founder's vision which may, for the sake of simplicity, be described as growing in love of both God and neighbour. So important is this vision that the individual's bottom line – no matter how high or low his position – is judged by how well he has accorded to it. And the bottom line of the community is the same; it stands to be judged by the same love. The very nature of this vision is potentially a powerful welder of community. Implicit in the founder's vision is that its market share should increase indefinitely through communicating the desirability of the principal vision through word and example.

The details of this vision are set out in Revelation through Scripture and Tradition. Its fullness has developed, and continues to develop, over time through the understanding and experience of the community, each one of whom is personally infused with the spirit of the vision. However the office holders, the Magisterium, have a special call to clarify the vision for all, and to protect it from contamination. The vicar of the founder, and the chief bishop, is the Pope, who has a special office of protecting the vision and proclaiming its essentials. Although he is, so to speak, a human managing director with a divine chairman, there is a guarantee – not that he will always proclaim the vision perfectly, but that he will never depart from the essentials of the vision, nor will the community.

Originally, soon after the founder had left them, the community was very small and was led by a handful of the founder's direct delegates, amongst whom he had appointed a kind of vicar with the office of holding the community together and strengthening it. Over the centuries the community has become extremely large and needs a multinational network of organization and control. It holds that the present management structure is essentially the same as the founder left it, but extended in various ways to deal with size and complexity. The bishops, for instance, are successors to the founder's original delegates, and the chief bishop is successor to the vicar.

This widespread community operates in relatively self-contained units, each called a diocese, under a bishop. The bishop is in some ways like the general manager of a territory of a business – but with an important difference. He holds his office directly from the divine chairman and not from the vicar. However, the bishop must work within the vision which the vicar protects. This whole executive group also has the function of acting as a college of universal leadership, which is never complete without the subscription of the vicar, who also has the constitutional authority to act on his own.

An important value in this context is the autonomy of every individual within the community. This derives initially from his dignity as a human being, but within the community it is enhanced by the fact that each one is infused directly with the spirit of the founder and is called personally to follow that spirit. He is held responsible for the ways in which he carries out the vision of the founder, and no one, not even the vicar, can relieve him of this. Indeed the vicar himself accepts the same autonomy and the same responsibility. While there is an analogy between this and the operation of a modern business, it goes much deeper. In business, autonomy and responsibility is at the behest of the chief executive; in the Church it is at the behest not of the vicar but of the founder – although of course the vicar teaches and supports the principle. Nor is it confined to the senior management of the community: it is central to the life of each member.

Naturally members of the community fall short of the vision from time to time. Indeed no one, once old enough to make such decisions, can claim never to have fallen short (with the exception of the founder and his mother). It is also possible, and not infrequent, in such a widespread and demanding environment, for individuals to repudiate the vision completely for a time, or indefinitely. However, the Church has a procedure which enables all individuals to regret their faults and to obtain forgiveness for them. It may be required for them to put right harm they have done through accepting a (generally) mild sanction or making restitution. There is no upper limit to the times this can be done. And in line with its founder's wishes there is a constantly positive attitude to those who fall short. Only in extreme and public cases does the Church exclude members of the community, although reconciliation and return to the community is always offered. There are various other sanctions, from censure to depriving office holders of their functions, which can be used.

The Church has a legal system within which it acts, called the Code of Canon Law. Originally a body of law built from different sources in the Middle Ages, it was codified and revised twice in the twentieth century. But it still bears the stamp of its long history.

Consequently the Church holds that subsidiarity is a fundamental principle – not only in secular communities but also in its own community. This is an exercise of the tight–loose principle well validated in other organizations. The Magisterium has the authority and the duty to govern the Church and to witness to the vision of the founder through its teaching. This includes the clarification and the execution of the vision, as well as correcting departures from it which may occur from time to time. But the principle of subsidiarity requires that the power of this authority should only be used when strictly necessary; as far as possible the autonomy of the members at all levels should be respected and enhanced. Ordinarily it should operate through influence and example, always seeking to inspire rather than to command.

This brief description, which might form the introduction to a management consultant's report, is accurate as far as it goes, although the writer would have missed the full depth which a believer might have caught. In particular, prayer life and the Sacraments, notably the Eucharist as an expression of unity, have not been described. The consultant would conclude that the Church is not only in line with modern understanding but also transcends it in many respects. And this would not be surprising because the Church is about loving relationships – man to God and man to man. In good businesses the concern which exists between the members can sometimes be appropriately described as love, but in the secular context love is a lubrication which facilitates the achievement of business goals; for the Church love is the goal.

But I would be on my guard. Effusive introductions to management consultants' reports are often the precursor of the severe qualifications which follow. The existence of the principles and structures of an organization do not necessarily coincide with the practice. Is, or to what extent might, the Church be making claims which are not verified in practice? That the Church up until recent history was, like most businesses, authoritarian is, I hope, common ground. We are more interested in the reforms which Vatican II brought about since its intention was to allow light and fresh air into the dusty corners, and with what has happened since. History is of course relevant in helping us to understand the culture into which the Council decrees were received and which may, as it might in any organization, have affected its reception.

Subsidiarity as a Principle for Change

I want to return to this issue because it is central to my theme. As far as I know the concept was first identified in 1931 by Pius XI in *Quadragesimo Anno* as a principle of the social order. It appeared in the same context in John XXIII's 1961 encyclical *Mater et Magistra*. It is reasonable to infer that the Church, seen as a social organization, should be subject to the same principle. However, that inference was explicitly confirmed by Pius XII in an address to new cardinals in 1946:

> Our Predecessor of happy memory, Pius XI, in his Encyclical on the social order 'Quadragesimo Anno', drew from this line of thought a practical conclusion and enunciated a principle of universal validity: what single individuals, using their own resources, can do of themselves, must not be removed and given to the community. This principle is equally valid for smaller and lesser communities in relationship to larger or more powerful communities. And the wise Pope [i.e Pius XI] goes on to explain, 'This is true because all social activity by its nature is subsidiary; it should serve as a support for the members of the social body and never destroy them or absorb them.' These words are indeed illuminating. They apply to all levels of life

in society as well as to the life of the Church, without prejudice to her hierarchical structure.[5]

So subsidiarity is a clear expression of the tight–loose structure which informs effective modern businesses. The 'loose' refers to granting and encouraging maximum autonomy of action, and the 'tight' refers to the residual power which remains in the hierarchy of the organization, although the onus of proof of need lies with the user of this power. And there's the rub. In secular organizations subsidiarity often proves hard to achieve because it is so easy to rationalize decisions to continue centralized control. And inevitably there will be some mistakes or irresponsibilities which occur – particularly in the early stages – which serve to confirm those who advocate centralization. Sometimes the degree of autonomy allowed to lower layers is so constrained as to be almost invisible. This does not of course inhibit the management from claiming that it operates on these principles. The fashionable concept of 'empowerment' can cover a range from wide autonomy to the ability only to make the most trivial of decisions within severely circumscribed limits. Or it may be a belief that management, seeing the business from a higher and broader vantage point, will always know better than the little people on the ground. The tendency to hang on to power is funda-mentally the same as the locked antlers of stags in the rutting season. It is the complementary characteristic to our instinct for obedience which I discussed in Chapter 4. Only people of emotional maturity and personal confidence are likely to release power to others, and these qualities are far from universal.[6] Lord Acton's famous dictum about the tendency of power to corrupt was written in the context of the absolutism of the Renaissance popes.[7] However, in secular business the need for better results or improvement in labour relations is likely to have a moderating effect on rule by power rather than influence. The Church does not have the advantage of such checks if she interprets the decline in her market as the fault of the market rather than of her approach to it.

Another feature of subsidiarity which can cause problems is that it contains a degree of ambiguity which is avoided in an organization with a tight rule book and clear laid-down procedures. The boundaries between levels in the hierarchy become more fuzzy, and so do peer boundaries. And the degrees of tightness and looseness may need to vary from time to time as circumstances change. People find it difficult to deal with ambiguity – particularly if they are psychologically immature. This is one of the reasons why cults which make high and absolutist demands can be attractive to people for whom clarity and certainty are major values. Subsidiarity depends much more on relationships than on rules. It is fundamentally dependent on good communication, travelling upwards, downwards and sideways. Such communication builds the trust needed to handle change and ambiguity, and of course to create intelligent participation in the goals of the organization.

Another important difference from secular autonomy may be noted. In business subsidiarity may be applied simply for pragmatic reasons – it makes the organization more successful. But in the Church it is recognized as a principle deriving from human nature – a principle in fact derived from the natural law. The archetype of subsidiarity is of course that God grants us freewill. The constraint is that he gave us the capacity to distinguish between good and evil, and the influence was provided by sending us his son, when we had already shown our capacity to flout his law, to call us and help us to live up to the true purposes of our lives within the community he had founded.

The principle can easily be misunderstood. This appears to have happened at the 2001 Synod of Bishops when Cardinal Bergoglio, who held official position, declared: 'The singular hierarchical structure of the Church, existing by the will of Christ, excludes an application of the principle of subsidiarity to the Church in the way in which it is intended and applied in sociology.' 'Subsidiarity', it was suggested, in Robert Mickens's report on the Synod,[8] has become a code word for 'shared authority' while 'communion' has become a code word for 'centralization'. But subsidiarity is not a republican or democratic ideal, as Pius XII showed in his phrase 'without prejudice to her hierarchical structure'. It says nothing about the power held at different levels, only about how that power is used. Its application will vary from one type of institution to another and even, when circumstances change, within the same institution.

A similar distortion appears when communion is equated with centralization. As Nicholl's account shows, communion and community depend on communication as a primary binding mechanism. A centralized authority communicating only downwards creates community only in the sense that unity created by the force of authority can create a unity. And inevitably it does so in so far as those who do not subscribe fully or partially to this authority *ipso facto* exclude themselves, or would, in the Church's terms, 'no longer be in full communion with the Catholic Church'.[9]

Subsidiarity and the Bishops

The bishops hold office in their own right as successors to the Apostles (that is, they are not delegates of superior authority as would be the case for senior executives in a business). They have ordinary and immediate jurisdiction in their diocese in their own right. However, this personal power is ultimately controlled by the supreme authority of the Church.[10] Immediately we have an ambiguity because although the structure conforms to subsidiarity, the balance, or the tension, between tightness and looseness can vary. In the first millennium of the Church the bishops ran on a relatively loose rein. Supreme authority tended to confine its power to an ad hoc basis either to deal with major issues or in relation to ecumenical councils. From the eleventh century onwards Papal power was exercised in an increasingly monarchical way so that the universal Church could be seen as one huge diocese which the Pope needed the delegated help of his bishops to rule. The First Vatican Council, in defining the powers of the Pope, was forced by external circumstances to break up before the powers of the bishops had been considered. This gave a one-sided view which was corrected at the Second Vatican Council, although the true position of the bishops was already well established.[11]

Notwithstanding the clarity of the bishop's personal jurisdiction it appears that there remains a strongly centralizing tendency at headquarters. Many advocates of this tendency remain, and they are often in powerful and influential positions. Archbishop Weakland of Milwaukee had his knuckles sharply rapped by the Vatican Congregation for Divine Worship for his proposal to re-order the layout of his cathedral. His opponents say that he has simply chosen to be disobedient. Weakland claims that he has broken no liturgical rules and takes the view that if ordinary and immediate jurisdiction does not extend to this, what does it extend to? The same Congregation published a massive instruction on how the liturgy should be translated into local languages (*Liturgiam Authenticam*, 2001). The document, all 33 articles and 86 footnotes, provided in great detail exactly how it should be done. This was after the ICEL[12] had been working for many years within the norms for translation of the liturgy set out by the Holy See in 1969. While not on the face of it attempting to remove the jurisdiction of bishops' conferences over translations of the liturgy the instruction was in effect setting out the norms which would have to be followed if the necessary acceptance of them was to be obtained. Following considerable controversy the Pope, in an address to the Congregation for Divine Worship, gave the instruction his personal endorsement.[13] I do not want to get into a liturgical argument (I am no liturgist) but the instruction seems to be a good example of negating proper subsidiarity without appearing to do so.[14]

The bishops also act collectively as a college vested with the powers of the Church to govern and teach. The Pope, as bishop of Rome, is a member of the college and because of his primacy it is not complete and cannot act with full authority without his consent. Bishops are not merely his advisers (as their secular equivalents might be) for their shared overall responsibility for the Church is of divine origin. Collegiality can be executed in different ways. Vatican II was an inspiring example of its formal use and value to the Church. It is also a more complete sign of the Church acting as a community than the Pope acting on his own. Less formally it exists through the general agreement of the bishops throughout the world exercising in community with the Pope the 'ordinary and universal magisterium'.[15]

The encyclical *Ordinatio Sacerdotalis* declaring definitively that the Church had no power to ordain women was later certified by the Congregation for the Doctrine of the Faith to be infallible in the light of this magisterium. However, it is not clear how it was established that this doctrine was so widely held by the bishops of the world since no consultation seems to have taken place. The truth of the doctrine is not an issue in this context, nor is the fact that a Curial congregation cannot declare infallibly that something is or is not infallible. It appears simply to be a manoeuvre – often used in secular business – to claim that there is broad agreement with an unpopular decision without carrying out the proper consultation. Nor does proper consultation appear to have taken place with regard to *Liturgiam Authenticam* despite its obvious effect on episcopal jurisdiction. The question of artificial contraception was withdrawn from consideration by the Council. There were doubtless good reasons for this but it gives the impression that someone was afraid the Council might decide it in 'the wrong way', or at the least show the split in the Magisterium on the matter. The Papal Commission set up to make recommendations then recommended the 'wrong way', and the Pope, as he was entitled to do, refused the recommendation. The ensuing encyclical could as easily have been written as if the Commission had never sat. But at least no one could say that popes never consult.

A similar spirit is shown in the Synod of Bishops which is held from time to time. Clearly this is a major opportunity for the Magisterium to reflect on aspects of the Church based on their insights and experience and to demonstrate its collegial nature – as the Council expected it to do.[16] Yet under headquarters' rules the agenda is set by the Pope, written submissions must be made several weeks beforehand, and there is very limited opportunity for debate. The Pope does not issue the recommendations of the synod until after the bishops have gone home. All documents and deliberations are kept confidential. It is a delicious irony that the Secretary of the Asian Synod (1998), Cardinal Schotte, required the Asian bishops to avoid the word 'subsidiarity' in their propositions, and, as I noted above, the concept received unfavourable comment in the Synod of

2001. A report on this Synod described the underlying current as reflecting 'an overwhelming desire of bishops for change within the Church, so that they might have a greater say in its day-to-day running'.[17] There were requests that the Synod, which was seen as a barely consultative body, should be given deliberative powers, and that local or national Episcopal Conferences, smartly called to heel previously by the Pope,[18] should be more fully recognized for the importance of their office in the Church.

If there is one group of people most likely to frustrate and demotivate senior executives in business it is the staff of the chief executive. There is always the temptation to increase personal staff in order to keep the executive lions at bay or to make time for more important things. There are in fact no more important things than dealing with the lions face to face. If increase in staff genuinely allows the chief executive to talk to the people who matter in the business then it may be justified, but it must be firmly controlled. The most dangerous tendency in headquarters staff is to believe for a moment that since they speak for the chief executive they are, or ought to be, more important than the executives who outrank them, or who have an authority which is independent of them. Another danger is that of forming an insulating blanket to manage – or rather prevent – communication between executives and the chief executive. It is essential for the chief executive to realize how often his name will be taken in vain, or how often he will be asked for routine confirmation of a staff decision the full significance of which he does not have time to grasp. The exasperation and the consequent inefficiency arising is bad enough in business. It is even worse in politics where democratically elected politicians find they are the cat's paws of influential forces, sometimes called a 'kitchen cabinet', close to the big chief. If murder is not done it must often be contemplated. I trust the diocesan bishops do not contemplate murder where the Curia is concerned, but the temptation must be strong for in this case the bishops hold their office from God while the Curia only has the delegated authority of his vicar.

The Roman Curia as a Curb on Subsidiarity

From the first the Apostles recruited outside assistance for their work, and this gradually developed and formalized over time until, by the eleventh century, the term 'Roman Curia' was first used. Today it has a number of congregations and tribunals, and its staff is of the order of 2,000. It is a very complicated grouping based on traditional models, and difficult for the outsider to understand. The Council asked that it should be reformed to make it more representative of the Church as a whole, to be more open in its listening to the Church – from diocesan bishops to members of the laity, and to review the appropriateness of its procedures.[19] Edward Schillebeeckx, then a theological expert in attendance at the Council, said: 'Many bishops were less concerned with a renewal of theology than with breaking the power of the Curia, which considered itself above the bishops.'

How have the reforms gone since then? Cardinal König, writing in the *Tablet* (27 March 1999), said: 'In fact, however, *de facto* and not *de jure*, intentionally or unintentionally, the curial authorities working in conjunction with the Pope have appropriated the tasks of the episcopal college. It is they who carry out almost all of them.' Looking at the thirty-four years between Schillebeeckx's observation and König's verdict one is reminded that the mills of God grind slowly, though it is a surprise to see them turning backwards. There has been some introduction of fresh blood into the Curia but it has not had the desired effect. As I noted above, authoritarian institutions have a self-reproducing quality. There is a tendency to recruit those of like mind, and rapidly to sandpaper off any remaining rough spots that prevent new members from being smoothly integrated into the group. Changing the culture of a long-established group requires strong leadership by someone who is determined to succeed. It takes time, ingenuity and a capacity to absorb attacks from powerful factions.

Communication does not appear to be the Curia's strong point. On one occasion the Congregation for the Doctrine of the Faith mentioned, as an example of a definitive teaching, the invalidity of

Anglican Orders. This came as a shock to the Archbishop of Westminster, the late Cardinal Hume. How would the Congregation have known what a sensitive matter this might be? The answer to that is: by routine consultation on key documents. By January 2002 even Pope John Paul felt constrained to urge the Congregation to use wider consultation before publishing its documents. (I understand that the terms of this exhortation were actually drafted by the Congregation itself – a delicious irony.)[20] But, as we have seen in other examples, the Curia provides little downwards communication (as opposed to instructions). A group of American canonists visiting the Vatican found that they were being quizzed by one section of the Curia on what another section might be doing. There seemed to be no other way to find out – so apparently there is little lateral communication either.

The appointment of diocesan bishops and lay people to the congregations and councils of the Curia has to some extent taken place, although the appointment of lay people has been very sparse. However, since one American cardinal reported that he had never been asked to attend a meeting of the congregation, and Archbishop Quinn of Chicago was only consulted three times – and then by post, there seems to have been more form than substance. There is little upwards communication. So the three routes of communication – downwards, upwards and sideways – are largely absent from headquarters. If we had no other evidence this alone would demonstrate that the subsidiarity of authority which the Church herself asserts as a requirement of the natural law is lacking in practice too.

No wonder that Killian McDonnell is able to quote no fewer than eight cardinals who have spoken out more or less explicitly on the need for restoring the proper role of episcopal authority.[21] Cardinal Kasper tells us: 'For all these reasons, the relationship between the universal and the local Church has become unbalanced. This is not just my own experience but the experience and complaint of many bishops around the world.'[22]

The Appointment of Bishops

Since the diocesan bishop will hold office in his own right in the area in which he is appointed, common sense would suggest that the local community – clergy and laity, as well as the local conference of bishops – should have a major say in who should be chosen. While the Pope as head of the episcopal college must have the ultimate right of approval it would be so unusual for a candidate to be rejected that it would be taken as a papal vote of no confidence.

This is not how it is done.

The bishops of the province collectively, or individually, send a regular report on those within their territories who might be suitable. But at the time of election it is the papal nuncio (the Pope's representative) who takes soundings from the local bishops, and such others as he may see fit. The depth of soundings is very much at his discretion, and in practice varies greatly. The nuncio then sends his own, secret, list to the Pope who is free to accept any or none of the proffered candidates.[23] This method may, for all I know, have produced the best diocesan bishops around – and the procedure was certainly introduced to control abuses, particularly interference from secular authority. But at the very least it conveys to the diocese the idea of a leader imposed rather than chosen. It would not be surprising if some suspected that the headquarters candidate – one assumes that the Curia have some influence here – was sometimes selected for ecclesio-political rather than objective reasons.

At the Synod of 2001 it was officially declared that the 'inadequate and arbitrary methods employed in the election of bishops' was not up for discussion.

Consulting the Laity

This issue of asking the laity to take part in the decision to proffer a candidate for consecration as their bishop raises the question of how subsidiarity applies to the laity. Who are the laity: pew-fillers, piggy banks, obedient peasants? No, says the Council, they are, first, priests, bringing their whole lives as an offering to God. Second, prophets, bearing witness by word and example to the truths of salvation both within their own family and to the outside world in which they move. Third, kings, sharing Christ's royal freedom to bring themselves and the world into the Kingdom.[24] St Paul, in speaking of the body of the Church, emphasizes its radical equality: everyone has received the same Spirit; no part can say of another, 'I have no need for you'; those parts which may seem less honourable should, for that reason, be treated with greater honour.[25] St Augustine speaks of his office as a bishop and his status as a Christian: 'The former is a danger; the latter is salvation.'[26] So in the Church everyone from Pope to pew is in the infantry; some, in addition, hold an office of service; but everyone earns the same campaign medal. The duty of the laity calls them to reveal their needs and desires and even on occasions to be critical for the good of the Church. Correspondingly the pastors must listen.[27]

So what does consulting the laity mean? In the immediate sense of the word it means that members of the laity have skills which the Church needs – from fund raising to medical science to demographics – and so on. This is the laity as secular expert, serving the practical needs of the organization. Other official channels of lay collaboration are roles such as lay ministers of the Eucharist or catechists. Here the Holy See goes to great lengths to ensure that the distinction between the laity and the clergy is sharply delineated.[28] But there is another sense of consultation which Newman was at pains to define in *On Consulting the Faithful in Matters of Doctrine* (1859). This is not asking the laity for advice or for their vote; it is recognizing that it is the whole Church which believes, and the whole Church includes the laity. The Magisterium has never, and could never, invent a single doctrine; it can only declare, with various degrees of authority, what the community believes. And the lowliest pew fodder can witness to his own belief as well as the highest ecclesiast. So the Magisterium, Newman taught, had better take the temperature of the laity in matters of faith. And he instances (though 'instance' does not seem quite the word in the light of Newman's capacity for multiple examples) that it was the laity who kept witness to the truth of the Incarnation when the bulk of the bishops championed Arianism. Even the Pope, under extreme pressure, was briefly induced to accept it. This is not a matter simply of listening to lay experts – such as those who sat on the Birth Control Commission – but the ear to the ground and the watchful eye which indicate what the laity believe by what they say and by what they do. And then asking, with some humility, is this the faith of the Church? Is it possible that the people see truths which are obscure to us?

It goes without saying that taking the laity's temperature requires prudence and discernment. It is easy to find factions with their own agendas, which cover a wide range of doctrinal beliefs or emphases; it is easy to find factions who have been so absorbed by the values of secular society that their Catholicism is little more than a label; it is easy to find factions whose beliefs are self-generated. But with deep and continuous listening it does become possible to separate the wheat from the chaff. What is the Christian experience of marriage? How do young Catholics experience the Church? What is it like to be Catholic and homosexual? How does it feel to be denied the priesthood because of one's gender? How does one combine the demands of business with the demands of charity? The questions multiply and the less welcome the answers the more important it is to hear them. In listening to the witness of good people, the truth – and sometimes a truer truth than the propositions of the Catechism – can be heard. 'It is precisely in communion with the Spirit-indwelt local community that the bishop is nourished in the apostolic tradition. His teaching authority is not delegated by the flock but is grounded in his relation to it.'[29]

Ironically, accepting the fact that one does not know all the answers can be the beginning of wisdom. I need hardly remind anyone that Socrates made that point a long time ago.

I am not qualified to give a verdict on how well the community listens to the laity. There are plenty of media from the correspondence columns of the newspapers to the Internet to various organizations set up at parish, diocesan or even Vatican level.

Valuable though these may potentially be they are likely to reflect the views of the articulate Catholic with an agenda. Other forums for listening are the private conversation of the confessional, the church porch, or the home visit. They may yield a deeper picture but there is the danger that respect for the clergy inhibits the discussion of difficult subjects – it is now the shorn lamb who tempers the wind to the tonsured shepherd. The clergy who are directly involved in pastoral activity have – forgetting a few backwoodsmen – an understanding of how the laity experience life and witness in the Church. But they are themselves manacled by official teaching. Every office holder from the highest down to parish priests, deacons and professors of theology and philosophy in seminaries have solemnly to accept the Profession of Faith[30] which includes: 'I also firmly accept and hold each and every thing that is proposed by that same church definitively with regard to teaching concerning faith or morals. What is more, I adhere with religious submission of will and intellect to the teachings which either the Roman pontiff or the college of bishops enunciate when they exercise the authentic Magisterium even if they proclaim those teachings in an act that is not definitive.' If you felt strongly that women should be ordained, or had a serious need to talk about the use of contraception in your marriage, would you be in a hurry to discuss these with a priest who only has a choice between the 'orthodox' line or breaking his solemn word?

So there are a number of one-way valves or filters in operation. The instructions come down from the top, or from near the top, but the response, the reaction and the witness of the laity, are filtered out by the successive layers through which they have to pass. Accordingly there is no apparent response, no visible sign that those who have the office of proclaiming the faith have understood it better and more fully as a result of listening to the faith of the laity.

Arthur Jones, editor at large for the *National Catholic Reporter* of Kansas City, reports on the disenchantment of American Catholics with their hierarchy. He tells us that 'They operate only in Rome's interests' and have capitulated on a number of sore issues. Meanwhile, American lay Catholics 'are not going away – not from the Church, that is, whereas they have moved away from its leadership'.[31] But our management consultant would have expected this; a lack of subsidiarity at the top creates pressures which make it even harder to sustain lower down.

The Parish Priest

This is someone who, being the equivalent of middle management, is to the secular eye in an unenviable position. His powers are delegated to him by the bishop, he does not hold them in his own right.[32] To the north of him is his bishop, free to direct him with whatever degree of subsidiarity he wishes; to the south is his parishioner to whom he has to minister directly, and of whose cares, worries and complaints he has to bear the brunt. Naturally these priests reflect in themselves a wide range of theological and authoritarian attitudes. Some are very conservative (not necessarily the oldest among them) and some are very progressive (not necessarily the youngest among them). Yet all of them are required by their office and their vow to present the same outward face of ecclesiastical solidarity. It has been noticed that middle managers suffer from substantially more stress than senior managers; the squeeze between north and south leaves the man in the middle feeling squashed flat.[33] The haemorrhage of priests and the shortage of vocations which persists has multiple causes[34] but the middle-management squeeze in a community which is ambivalent about its identity would be expected to make a major contribution.

It follows of course that the bishop should exercise the principle of subsidiarity with regard to his priests, although they do not, as he does, hold their office by divine right. A recent report on priests' morale from an English diocese mentions, among other problems, 'priests are frightened to death to tell the truth' and 'a lack of transparency in (diocesan) decision-making'.[35] This is not surprising: the conduct of authority from the top strongly influences the conduct of authority throughout the echelons. On current projections this diocese will lose 40 per cent of its priests over the ten years following the survey. It may be, however, that the support for this investigation from the diocesan bishop indicates an openness to upwards communication, however painful, which will enable many matters to be put right.

Implied Contracts

A common feature of organizations is that implied contracts exist, and for all their informality they cannot be broken with impunity. One implied contract is that the Church will be truthful in its dealings. This is not just a question of falsehood; it includes any attempt to mislead or even lack of due frankness, irrespective of the motive. It would, for instance, be difficult to glean from *Humanae Vitae* that the Papal Commission by a substantial majority recommended that the Church's teaching should change. There is no reference in the Council Declaration on Religious Liberty that a complete volte face from the previously held position had taken place.[36] At an important meeting Pope John Paul declared that the Holy See 'has always been vigorous in defending freedom of conscience and religious liberty'.[37] Unless some strong qualifications to this statement went unreported there are a few heretics who would raise a scorched eyebrow at that.

It is often proclaimed, that – in contrast to many other denominations – the Catholic Church does not permit divorce. In fact this is not true. The Pope has power to divorce a marriage provided it has not been consummated even if one of the parties is unwilling. This is not an annulment – a true marriage (like that of Mary and Joseph) has taken place and the Pope dissolves the bond. Secondly a marriage between unbaptized people can be dissolved if one party decides to be baptized and the other party is unwilling to leave peaceably in this situation. Called the Pauline Privilege, the former marriage is dissolved by the making of the second marriage. Although the Privilege is exercised 'in favour of the faith' the new partner does not, with the bishop's permission, actually have to be baptized.[38] Thirdly the Petrine Privilege, which strangely does not appear in Canon Law, enables the Pope to dissolve any valid marriage, consummated or not, provided one of the partners was not baptized. It has often been exercised, and in a wide range of circumstances.[39] To the outside eye, it looks a little as if the Church makes her own exceptions to suit herself but then keeps quiet about them.

This is a different issue from the common situation in which someone baptized as a Catholic marries outside the Church, and later wishes to marry someone else. Notwithstanding the good faith of the first partner – and quite possibly the good faith of the Catholic at the time of the first marriage – the Church will regard it as void and permit the 'second' marriage with full Catholic honours. The reasons for this are clear cut. The Church is merely saying that the first union was not a marriage for the Catholic and therefore there is no marriage bond. A purely legal question. But the Church is not a purely legal community. The Catholic party has made a solemn promise and has now – with or without good reason – broken it. And the partner has relied on that promise. Again it looks like one rule for Catholics and another for everyone else. At the very least there should be some indication in the solemnization of the Catholic marriage that something regrettable has happened.

The Magisterium clearly distinguishes divorce and annulment. Nevertheless the grounds for annulment are now so broad that it is possible to argue, as some canon lawyers do, that it should always be possible to establish a basis for annulling a marriage whenever it has irretrievably broken down.[40] Certainly anecdotal evidence from those concerned with the process suggests that this is in practice true. Many will argue that this is an ingenious way to enable mercy to be shown in deserving cases without breaching the Church's prohibition on divorce. But we must not be surprised if others see an element of having your cake and eating it.

Garry Wills gives us a broad historical picture in his book *Papal Sin: Structures of Deceit.*[41] One does not have to agree with the interpretation or the account of every incident he discusses to infer that the Church has, almost as an instinctive habit, closed ranks in the face of scandal, hoped that her more grotesque historical teachings or behaviour would be quietly forgotten, and used her skill to demonstrate how doctrine, which to the ordinary mind has simply been changed, is really a development of a previous understanding. Wills argues that these are not just instances but have become grafted into the structures of the Church. He does not use the phrase 'institutionalized economy with the truth', but that's his documented drift.

The tendency to rewrite the past or to maintain a low profile on current practices which might cause a flutter in the dovecotes is, at worst, a characteristic of a totalitarian regime and at best what has come to be called, in English political comment, 'spin'. It has no place in the Church of God, but once the habit is established it becomes increasingly difficult to retreat. Such behaviour would of course be immensely damaging to a business. Morale may be preserved by shading the truth for a time but the price is eventual disillusion and loss of trust. It makes authority temporarily a little easier to sustain but in the end authority is forfeited. The basic principle that the end does not justify the means is defied at one's peril.

In Pope John Paul's encyclical for the Jubilee Year 2000, *Tertio Millennio Adveniente*, there is an expression of repentance for 'intolerance and even the use of violence in the service of truth' at times in the Church's history. In the paper produced to comment on and extend this the International Theological Commission noted: 'Indeed, in the entire history of the Church there are no precedents for requests for forgiveness by the Magisterium for past wrongs. Councils and papal decrees applied sanctions, to be sure, to abuses of which clerics and laymen were found guilty, and many pastors sincerely strove to correct them. However, the occasions when ecclesiastical authorities – Pope, Bishops, or Councils – have openly acknowledged the faults or abuses which they themselves were guilty of, have been quite rare.' This paper, following the Pope, tells us that the 'understanding of the past is translated into its application to the present'.[42] These documents refer to behaviour inconsistent with Christianity rather than mistaken doctrine, and are far from complete. But they are at least a start.

Another important implied contract in business is that all employees will be treated justly, particularly in disciplinary matters. Indeed in most civilized jurisdictions there will be legal protection of employee rights. The better businesses did not need the law; they knew that they could only trust their employees if their employees could trust them. A recent account of a number of individuals who have come up against the Church's discipline suggests that its grasp of good employment practice, to say nothing of basic human rights, leaves a great deal to be desired.[43] The *Oxford Companion to Christian Thought* (2001), in discussing the case of Father Balasuriya (a Sri Lankan priest who was excommunicated for his theological views and reconciled after making a profession of faith), describes the authorities' response as showing an 'extraordinary disregard for natural justice and due process of law'. Michael Walsh reports himself as struck 'by the plain and simple discourtesy displayed by the CDF. The books which are under censure are not properly read; letters go unanswered; those accused are rarely approached personally, but through their superiors. Balasuriya learned of his excommunication when he heard a BBC broadcast.'[44] For a Church which is centred on the message of love for God and man to have to look outside at secular practice to learn how to treat people with basic human decency seems, to say the least, odd. The lack of respect for the rights of individuals is a characteristic of an organization whose management has not learnt to respect its subordinates.

Our management consultant would, I think, be faced by a difficult task. He will know from experience that a critical report will often bring a response that the consultants had failed to understand the business. So he might perhaps, with all appearance of humility, seek from the organization the answer to some issues which confuse him. They might be:

- Given that the Church believes that subsidiarity is a necessary principle of operation in organizations, and is demanded by the rightful autonomy of members, would the authorities describe how this is applied in practice at different levels and give examples of how it has developed since the Council?

- Given the evidence that many senior executives in the Church believe that their prerogatives are endangered by creeping centralization, would the authorities explain in what way these executives have misunderstood the situation?
- Given that the Vatican Council asked that the Roman Curia should be reformed, would the authorities explain what reforms have been introduced, and gauge their effectiveness?
- Given that the Church is a community of people who are radically equal, would the authorities describe the steps, consistent with the ultimate needs of order, which have been taken to reflect and give weight to the various categories within the community?
- Given that the Church describes herself as a community founded on love, would the authorities give instances of how they have promoted communication upwards, downwards and laterally; and how they have followed the principle of maximum freedom of information?
- Given that the Church holds truth to be a sacred principle, would the authorities demonstrate her commitment to truth notwithstanding the risk of embarrassment, and show how the apparent contradictory instances are misconceived?
- Given that the Church is committed to justice and love, would the authorities describe how their disciplinary procedures exhibit these virtues in both principle and practice?

Sincere and thoughtful answers to these questions would, I think, lead to a realization that, while the Church in its essential constitution is ordered to the autonomy of its members and the corresponding use of subsidiarity in its exercise of authority, practice has contradicted this. Our management consultant would know even without the benefit of Scripture that the real test of values is not words but deeds. And the results in the Church today suggest that this contradiction has been highly damaging. The next question would be to decide what to do about it. In a secular business the immediate step would be clear. And the more clearly and absolutely power has been claimed the more swiftly and radically would the necessary changes be made. But the Church, as the Pope reminds us, is not a mere secular organization and it has a unique constitution. For her the answers may need to be different.

Notes to Chapter 7

1. 20 November 1999.
2. The classic account of the contrasting approaches, known as X Theory and Y Theory, are described by Douglas McGregor in *The Human Side of Enterprise* (McGraw-Hill, 1960).
3. The best-known analysis of the hierarchy of human motivation is Abraham Maslow, 'A Theory of Human Motivation', *Psychological Review*, 50 (1943).
4. Donald Nicholl, 'The Layman and Ecclesiastical Authority', *Clergy Review* (July 1964). Professor Revans's study was later published as *Standards for Morale: Cause and Effect in Hospitals* (OUP, 1964). The study quoted is only part of a longer article of exceptional interest, and relevance to my theme. If you can get hold of a copy, read it and learn much.
5. I first encountered this passage in the lecture given by Archbishop John Quinn at Campion Hall, Oxford, England, in 1996. Quinn, now retired but formerly Archbishop of San Francisco, developed his lecture into a book called *The Reform of the Papacy* (Crossroad, 1999). Those who have read this book will know how much I, as no Vaticanologist, am indebted to it in this chapter, but he must not be held responsible for my interpretation and views on the subject. Quinn's purpose was to respond to the Pope's request, in his encyclical *Ut Unum Sint* (1995), for help to reform the office of the Papacy in the light of ecumenical need. http://www.ewtn.com/library/bishops/oxford.html, or search (e.g. Google) for John R. Quinn. You will also find a number of documents commenting favourably and unfavourably on both the lecture and the book, and there is clearly room for argument about the detail.
6. Dr Dominian, *Authority* (Burns & Oates, 1976), describes the authoritarian personality in some detail.

7. Letter to Bishop Mandell Creighton (3 April 1887).

8. *Tablet* (20 October 2001).

9. Commentary on *Ad Tuendam Fidem* by the Congregation for the Doctrine of the Faith (29 June 1998).

10. *Lumen Gentium* 27.

11. See Quinn, *Reform of the Papacy*, pp. 93ff. The essential doctrine of episcopal power was stated by the German bishops in 1875, and strongly confirmed by Pius IX in that year. Quinn, *Reform of the Papacy*, pp. 78ff.

12. International Commission on English in the Liturgy.

13. 21 September 2001.

14. The instruction has been heavily criticized by biblical and liturgical scholars for various howlers, including the failure of the Congregation to consult, as they were required to do, the Pontifical Biblical Commission. See for example Father John Fitzsimmons's letter, *Catholic Herald* (21 September 2001). The Pope made a strong statement in support of the instruction, *Catholic Herald* (26 October 2001).

15. Encyclical *Evangelium Vitae* (1995).

16. Vatican II decree *Christus Dominus* 5.

17. Report by Bruce Johnston in the *Catholic Herald* (2 November 2001).

18. Pope John Paul II, *Motu proprio*, 'On the Theological and Juridical Nature of Episcopal Conferences' (21 May 1998).

19. *Christus Dominus* 9, 10.

20. *Tablet* (26 January 2002).

21. 'Our Dysfunctional Church', *Tablet* (8 September 2001).

22. 'On the Church', *Tablet* (23 June 2001).

23. Canon 377.

24. *Lumen Gentium* 32ff.

25. 1 Cor. 12 *passim*.

26. Quoted in *Lumen Gentium* 32.

27. *Lumen Gentium* 37. The document asks that the laity's opinion should be expressed through official agencies. Some might argue, however, that this depends on this kind of communication being genuinely effective.

28. 'Instruction on Certain Questions regarding the Collaboration of the Non-ordained Faithful in the Sacred Ministry of Priest', 15 August 1997, issued jointly by several Curial Congregations.

29. David McLoughlin,'Authority as Service in Communion', in *Governance and Authority in the Roman Catholic Church* (SPCK, 2000), p. 132.

30. Canon 833.

31. 'The American Way', *Tablet* (15 June 2002).

32. Canons 519, 717.

33. Charles B. Handy, *Understanding Organizations*, (Penguin, 1981), p. 69.

34. A valuable survey of priests carried out in the Portsmouth diocese is reported in the *Tablet* (17 November 2001). Too long to summarize here, it broadly confirms my analysis. See also Timothy Radcliffe's address to NCP 2002 (*Tablet* 7 September 2002).

35. A report to the clergy formation team in the diocese of Portsmouth, and welcomed by the diocesan bishop. *Tablet* (17 November 2001).

36. Discussed in Charles E. Curran, *The Catholic Moral Tradition Today* (Georgetown University Press, 1999), p. 220.

37. Address to Ambassadors accredited to the Holy See, reported in the *Tablet* (20 January 2001). In Chapter 5, n. 11, I provide some documentation for earlier Papal attitudes.

38. Canons 1142–47.

39. Instruction of the Holy Office, 1 May 1934. This does not appear in the official record of the Holy See, but copies were forwarded to the Ordinaries at the time. Discussed, with case reports, in A. H. Van Vliet and C. G. Breed, *Marriage and Canon Law* (Burns & Oates, 1964), 491ff.

40. Timothy J. Buckley CSSR, 'English Catholics and Divorce', in M. P. Hornsby Smith, *Catholics in England 1950–2000* (Cassell, 1999).

41. Darton, Longman and Todd (2000).

42. *Memory and Reconciliation: The Church and the Faults of the Past* (December 1999).

43. Paul Collins, *From Inquisition to Freedom* (Continuum, 2001).

44. *Tablet* (24 March 2001), p. 418.

CHAPTER 8

THE COMMUNION OF THE CHURCH

I have chosen in this book to look first at the autonomy of the individual, arguing that the Church, in line with its own principles, should be encouraging and developing this autonomy. It would be seen most clearly in following through the meaning and consequences of the sovereignty of conscience. And this can best be done by teaching the process of conscience formation with the explicit recognition that the individual is always responsible for his decision even if it be at variance with the Magisterium. I have then suggested that this can only take place within an ecclesiastical structure which reflects its belief in autonomy at all levels. This must be achieved through the principle of subsidiarity, which is the corresponding response of authority to the requirement of autonomy.

Notwithstanding the strong lead given by Vatican II, the forces of resistance to this have been mustered, and work hard to maintain the dictatorial line. At one level these forces are successful – the Church becomes more and more centralized as time passes. At another they fail because the Catholic faithful diminish in their numbers and their practice, the influence of the Church in the world is fading – and the *reductio ad absurdum* of this trend would be a very small, tightly controlled, organization with no members.

Lest this *reductio* be thought to be altogether too *absurdum* it may be worth noticing that while the number of priestly vocations has halved since Vatican II, the number of bishops has doubled.[1] This is an interesting instance of Parkinson's Law which was developed from statistics such as the inverse ratio between the number of admiralty officials and the number of capital ships in the Royal Navy – although in this case the ratio was not so extreme.[2]

In its exercise of authority the Church is dogged by a disadvantage which is less likely to afflict secular organizations. It is relatively easy for these to establish a clear measurement of success. It may be bottom line, or market share, or growth in capital value, or achievement of specific objectives. And this means that when any of the chosen criteria are not achieved management is automatically put on warning that something is going wrong. A successful analysis of causes leads to an action plan which has the potential to get the business back on course. But the criteria for the Church are too slippery for that. Point at decrease of numbers and the defence is that quality is better than quantity. What can the Church do if the evil world or the fainthearted Catholic refuses her message? Point to sinfulness in the Church and the response is that we are distinguished by being a Church which can comprehend sinners. It is almost a matter of pride. Point to the over-centralization of authority, and the response is that, on the contrary, only firmer adherence to such authority will preserve the fidelity of the Church's message.

Pope John Paul, in line with Vatican II, constantly calls the Church to holiness. The Theological Commission reflects on this and says: 'Christians have the responsibility to live in such a way as to show others the true face of the living God. They are called to radiate to the world the truth that "God is love (*agape*)" ' (1 Jn 4. 8, 16). Since God is love, he is also a Trinity of Persons, whose life consists in their infinite mutual communication in love. It follows from this that the best way Christians can radiate the truth that God is love is by their own mutual love. "By this all will know that you are my disciples, if you love one another" (Jn 13. 35).'[3] Here at last we have a statement of ultimate criterion. But only for a fleeting moment – the Commission continues with a passage from *Gaudium et Spes* (19) taken somewhat out of context: 'For this reason, it can be said of Christians that often "to the extent that they neglect their own training in the faith, or teach erroneous doctrine, or are deficient in their religious, moral or social life, they must be said to conceal rather than reveal the authentic face of God and of religion".' With one stroke the Commission confuses the ultimate criterion set by Christ, with a secondary and indirect set of criteria which, perhaps only by coincidence, is exactly that of the centralist agenda.

I am not suggesting that these secondary criteria are unimportant. On the contrary, only a Church whose major recognizable characteristic is mutual love could hope to fulfil them. So let me return to the ultimate criterion set by Christ rather than by the Theological Commission.

A community of mutual love displays somewhat specific characteristics. First, it shares fundamental beliefs, values and objectives. Within the community – even one as small as a married couple – there are different functions and roles; but these exist for the service of other members and for the community as a whole. There is a welcomed acceptance of interdependence. Outside its core beliefs, indeed because of their strength, difference of views is not only possible but to some degree necessary. The community only advances through the dialectic of different perspectives and different understandings. Some of these emerge from the experience of different roles, some emerge from the diversity of gifts enjoyed by different members. The diversity is fruitful because it is welcomed and respected as a means of deeper understanding. Throughout, the atmosphere is one of care, respect and sharing in the common objectives.

Naturally, because of the weakness of human nature, there are flashpoints of disagreement. But respect remains and these disagreements are eventually resolved or reconciled through good communication. In fact communication is at the heart of a loving community. In marriage counselling one finds that problems with communication are ordinarily at the heart of the difficulties, and restoring communication is the source of their resolution. The couple may talk a good deal but they do not communicate. It is as if their self-centred aims cause them to speak a language the other does not understand. Communications require a sincere wish to understand how it is for the other person and to seek ways of harmonizing two, at least apparently, different perceptions. Harmony is the fruit of care and respect.

In Chapter 11 of Genesis the account of the Tower of Babel, historical or not, is a metaphor for how mankind through pursuing different and selfish ambitions in defiance of God lost the power of communication. They spoke different languages and could no longer understand each other. But Genesis moves on immediately to the introduction of Abraham and his mission – a restoration of communication through following the call of God. At the other end of the Bible we find the reverse of Babel in Paul's account which emphasizes that all the members of the body of the Church, differing in their roles and functions, are fed by the same spirit – and every member, however humble, is equal in Christ, interdependent and needed within the community. Transcending these differences is the power of love.[4]

Communication involves risk. To communicate you have to let down your drawbridge, and now the world can see you as you really are. That's scary. And the world can come in, forcing you to see other realities. Communication opens you to the possibility of change – and that is a well-founded fear because change is exactly what happens. So to communicate you have to trust the other, and the other has to trust you.

So the first and most obvious sign of mutual love within the Church is that real communication takes place. Upwards, downwards and sideways the members of the Church need to listen deeply, to understand how it is for each other. And, as I described in the previous chapter, the climate of this respectful and caring communication has to be initiated from the top. There are pockets of real communication in many places in the Church but, by and large, the community is not distinguished by its communication. By talk, yes; by instruction, yes; by exhortation, yes; by dispute, yes. By communication, no. And so the face of Christ is concealed.

But the analogy of marriage, hallowed though it is in Scripture, does not take us far enough because marriage does not – today at any rate – involve hierarchical authority. And this takes us straight back into the question I have looked at throughout this book – autonomy and subsidiarity – one coin with two sides.

It is common ground that authority within the Church is exercised by the Magisterium, and written into the title deeds by its founder. It has an essential role to preserve and teach the truths of Revelation, which constitute the core around which the community is formed. The deeper understanding and the application of Revelation results from the faith of the whole community. This may become apparent through any or all parts of the Church – the faithful, the theologians, the clergy. But the Magisterium has a gubernatorial office – a touch on the tiller to guide, a lowering of the anchor when rocks are near. There is no necessary incompatibility between the exercise of hierarchical authority and freedom. But in a listening community distinguished by mutual love the way in which that authority is exercised is all-important.

In the last chapter I quoted the view that subsidiarity has become a code word for 'shared authority' while 'communion' has become a code word for 'centralization'. And this distinction epitomizes the problem. There is a wholly understandable fear that shared authority leads to an unacceptable diversity of views and practice. Doctrine loses its hard-edged focus and through freedom of interpretation emerges with so many meanings that it has no meaning at all. Similarly, good order descends into confusion. After all, the loss of centralized authority in the sixteenth century led to a multitude of competing reformed Churches which have continued to multiply, and to create different factions within themselves. Once the cement of authority had been removed the house began to collapse into fragments. This cannot be what God wants for his Church.

But this of course has nothing to do with subsidiarity. Remember the tight–loose principle. Centralization is the tight principle in action; the Reformation was, ultimately if not immediately, the loose principle in action. Subsidiarity requires both: tight where it needs to be tight; loose wherever tightness is not strictly required. Although the balance between the two is hard to achieve, loose is the preferential option. It is preferred because it is only through the maximization of autonomy that the full gifts of the Spirit – given to every member – can be made available for the building and strengthening of the Church.

The key to reducing the need for compulsive authority is to replace it with leadership authority. Through the conviction and inspiration of the leadership the members of the community participate in the objectives autonomously. They *choose* to internalize the values and so to live them out. Dictatorial authority does not need leadership; leadership does not need dictatorial authority. But the leadership has to be clear about the essentials – those few things which really matter. And it must communicate these as far as possible by inspiration rather than demand. The outcome, of course, is that power is replaced by influence. And it is only through the influence of leadership that people seek to know more about their faith and to understand and teach true doctrine more fully and enhance their religious, moral and social life, and so exhibit the characteristics which the Theological Commission seeks to promote so the face of God can be more clearly seen. Again and again the history of human nature, and the more specific experience of modern business, confirms that it is leadership not power which is the most effective in the long run.

Of course the Magisterium, just as in secular management, does not lose any of its constitutional powers. These are used when needed, and only when needed, to take executive action. The occasions should be very rare – and all the more effective because of their rarity. However, authority in the Church must be continually aware of the temptation to claw back control at the expense of the autonomy of her members. The ease with which one may convince oneself that this or that command is necessary means that every potential instance should be challenged; the perennial temptation of institutions to retain psychological control over members through the use of guilt must be firmly resisted; the inclination of hierar-chical institutions towards totalitarianism must be recognized and fought; the struggle against the natural tendency of power to corrupt must be continuous. Whenever Moses let his hands fall the Israelites began to lose the battle against Amalek; whenever the Church fails to be on its guard against the abuse of its authority it begins to lose its battle for the freedom which Christ bought.

The principle of subsidiarity needs to be reflected in the whole way the Church works. Some of the changes which are necessary are discussed in Archbishop Quinn's book *The Reform of the Papacy*. I am much indebted to this book for many of the details and issues addressed in my previous chapter.[5] I yield to Quinn's far greater knowledge of these matters; and he himself proposes them for discussion rather than as definitive statements. In brief, he looks at collegiality in the Church, the appointment of bishops, the reforms of the Papacy, the College of Cardinals and the Roman Curia. His objective is to respond to the Pope's requests for ways in which reform in the Church would contribute to allowing non-Catholic Christians to recognize the presence of Christ in the Church. I was introduced to the kernel of his thought by a transcription of his key paper on the subject which is to be found on the Internet.[6] Quinn would have no difficulty in subscribing to the Pope's belief that: 'The best preparation for the new millennium, therefore, can only be expressed in a renewed commitment to apply, as faithfully as possible, the teachings of Vatican II to the life of every individual and of the whole Church.'[7]

Quinn's chosen purpose does not encompass the area of the individual conscience but I believe that from the background of broad ecclesiastical reform would emerge certain principles which would make the employment of the Church and Council's teaching on the autonomy of the individual a practical possibility. This does not mean that the Church should leave its non-infallible moral teaching as an open question. But it would recognize explicitly that she can only give her best understanding of the moral law. New scientific knowledge, new sets of assumptions, and deeper insights might lead to development or even revision. It has done so in the past and it is necessary to acknowledge that it may well do so in the future. Certainly a communicating Church, through the perceptions of the whole community, would be in a far stronger position to understand the truth more deeply, and get ever closer to the will of God.

I have lived all my life in the Catholic Church, and in it I hope to die. The most rewarding religious experience of my life occurred a short while ago as I was preparing for a serious operation with a small but definite risk of mortality. I made a general Confession before receiving the Anointing of the Sick, and in it we did not bother about a listing of sins. Instead we talked about whether I had loved enough the people who surround me. I will not share the details but, believe me, there was matter enough for Absolution. Afterwards my wife – the chief object of my imperfect human love – and I received the Eucharist togther. It brought me to terms with myself, and I went into the operating theatre with a deep sense of peace. I try now – fully recovered – to live up to the graces of the Sacrament. I do not do too well, but I do a little better. For me that was the face of Christ in the Church.

So that is the mark of the Church: 'By this all will know that you are my disciples, if you love one another.' Love within the community has to be worked out in all its elements and meaning. It is no wishy-washy sentimental ideal; it includes the positive expression of the Theological Commission's criteria – good training in the faith, the teaching of true doctrine and the development of the religious, moral or social life. But unless that is inspired and motivated by a true desire to lead every member of the community, whatever their role, towards their full autonomy as adult Christians – to be what they can be – then it is not love. Merely the sounding brass and the tinkling of cymbals.

Notes to Chapter 8

1. *Tablet* (9 June 2001), p. 847.
2. C. Northcote Parkinson, *Parkinson's Law* (John Murray, 1958).
3. *Memory and Reconciliation: The Church and the Faults of the Past* (December 1999).
4. 1 Cor. 12 and 13 *passim*.
5. Crossroad, 1999.
6. See Chapter 7, n. 5.
7. *Tertio Millennio Adveniente* (10 November 1994).

A LOOK AT DISSENT IN ACTION

It is useful to see how what might appear to be unchangeable moral positions begin to take on a different form in the light of greater secular knowledge. For example our developing understanding of the process of conception and embryonic development over the centuries has altered the perceived moral status of abortion.[1] The ban on usury fell into desuetude before a greater understanding of economics and the clear justice of receiving an appropriate return by way of interest. Aquinas in the thirteenth century, though no misogynist, thought a woman was, and I paraphrase, 'that which results when the conception of a man goes wrong'.[2] Noldin in the 1950s still taught the natural inferiority of women.[3] In such cases advancing secular knowledge can lead to correction of well-established teachings. It has been particularly interesting to observe this in areas where the Magisterium has identified sins against nature. I introduced this question in Chapter 2.

The vast majority of moral judgements, unlike sins against nature, are made through reason and call for rational assessment of the circumstances. While I accept the general principle of justice that I must not defraud labourers of their wages I need to apply it carefully to the situation. I can imagine some plausible, if unusual, circumstances when I might consider withholding wages – perhaps because I have evidence a worker has not fulfilled his undertaking or perhaps because I am going bankrupt and have to weigh up the different claims of several creditors. Similarly I must not tell a lie, because my neighbour has a right to the truth and I have an obligation in charity to give it. But there are circumstances where telling a lie might be justified; I give an example on page 26. Equally there are plenty of examples when I might not strictly tell a lie and yet culpably deceive. But the one area of morals in which such reasoned application has no place is sins against nature. The history of this is informative. The traditional authorities divided the natural law into two parts – that which was shared with the animal kingdom and therefore based on physical aspects, and that which was unique to human beings because it was based on reason. Of the two the physical element was the more important because it was written into our natures directly by God.

A benign example is the principle of totality which states that the parts of the body exist for the good of the whole. Therefore direct self-mutilation is always wrong unless it be required for the health of the whole body. But when the gift of a kidney by a live donor became an issue, moral theologians had some difficulty in squaring this with the original principle. Fortunately they were able to work their way around this. One method was by introducing the idea of 'functional' totality which seems to rest on the basis that God provided a second and unnecessary kidney just in case someone else should happen to need it. Another method was to justify it by 'fraternal charity' which seems to mean something like 'it stands to reason that organ donation is right; it's just that we haven't thought of the reason yet'. This is dangerously close to accepting that the commonsense demands of love might just outweigh the laws dictated by physical nature.[4]

But the great arena for sins against nature was the process of generation. This above all was the province of the natural or animal. Given to us directly by God its right conduct was written within its physical nature. A visitor from Mars considering the functioning of mammalian sexual biology would sensibly conclude that it was designed as a 'mechanism' to deposit seed in the female tract, and thus open to fertilize. Consequently he would see the interposition of a barrier to prevent the seed achieving its natural function as interfering with the physical end of the act. He might see the act as having other and social purposes, particularly where human mammals were concerned, but nevertheless the prevention of the act from fulfilling its capacity to fertilize would be a frustration of its physical design.

To the Martian this would be an academic observation, just as it would be for us if we were, for some reason, to make bulls use condoms or, as is routinely the case, to extract and store their seed for later use. But to the traditional teaching of the Magisterium it was a question of human beings directly interfering with a God-given faculty and therefore gravely wrong. Artificial contraception is a sin against nature and therefore, by definition, a perversion. There is no set of circumstances which could justify such a disruption of the moral order.[5] 'Just as the ordering of right reason proceeds from man, so the order of nature is from God Himself: wherefore in sins contrary to nature, whereby the very order of nature is violated, an injury is done to God, the Author of nature' wrote Aquinas – and such sins even in marriage are worse in his view than fornication or adultery, which, though wrong, were not seen as unnatural.[6] It was of course gradually (and I speak of centuries here) realized that intercourse in marriage had other direct purposes besides procreation and the 'rendering of the debt', until – to the disapproval of the old school – Pius XI gave formal approval to the use of the infertile period as a means of contraception, when the reasons for this were adequate.[7] This merciful remission underlined the fact that the prohibition was not essentially based on the avoidance of conception but on the physical perversion of the act itself. Biological structure not intention was the criterion.

It was inevitable that to medieval understanding the handwriting of God, and therefore his ordinance, would be seen in the physical design of the sexual act. After all did he not create it exactly in that way, leaving no area for doubt about its proper use? Well, no. We now understand about evolution and must look at the question in light of that. God does not create animal forms directly but allows them to develop through evolution favouring the characteristics which are suited to the survival of the species. It is plausible (though in the nature of things undocumented) that the rate of fertility needed for the survival of the human race was calibrated to the conditions in which the human race developed from its hominid ancestors. The calibration was no doubt crude but sufficiently well adapted to the tough conditions of the time to enable the race to reproduce itself and give a reasonable level of population increase needed for the work of survival. The characteristic of sexual desire at infertile times was presumably an adaptation supporting the need for parents to remain bonded during the long period of maturation required by human offspring. And the (usual) state of infertility during lactation gave some control over the natural interval between conceptions. So we must abandon the idea of God's direct instructions at the superficial level of anatomy and look to the deeper level of how God achieved his purposes through evolution. This of course does not mean that we should disregard the physical structures as they are. In the absence of a written instruction book we may be able to infer how an object should work from studying its structures. But if we start from seeing the development of sexual biology as a response to external and accidental conditions rather than a direct creation, we are open to consider whether the laws to be inferred from them are, so to speak, fixed for all eternity in the mind of God, or susceptible to review as the external conditions which brought them about changed.

These changing conditions are most starkly shown by looking at historical total fertility rates (TFR). The TFR is a calculation of the number of live births to the average female in a population over her reproductive life. A number of factors contribute to the TFR but the pattern is quite clear. In the USA the TFR in 1880 was around 7. Currently it is 2.0, roughly the figure required for the population of a developed country to reproduce itself in the next generation. What has happened is that the number of women living long enough to bear children has greatly increased as a result of higher standards of living and improving medicine. Today the USA does not need and could not easily sustain a TFR of 7. And so, by whatever means, American women have restricted their fertility to a more suitable figure.[8] Similar, and in many cases more extreme, patterns of reducing TFRs are to be seen in, for instance, Europe.[9] Currently countries with high TFRs are in underdeveloped regions and tend to have high infant mortality.

This looks like a process which is characteristic of the human race. By and large the animal kingdom continues to evolve physically against changing conditions. Or, if you wish, failure to evolve leads to extinction. Human beings do not evolve in the same way; they use their brain rather than their genes to adapt to changing conditions. So what we are seeing is an artificial correction to an outcome of evolution which served its purpose in the past but which has been overtaken by new circumstances. That does not mean that any method of controlling conception is morally acceptable. For example, abortifacients are ruled out of court by the principle that human beings are always to be treated as ends, and never as means. (I leave aside issues about when a *conceptus* becomes a human being because this does not affect the principle.) And clearly some people, for a variety of reasons, may want to use safe period methods. But that the use of artificial barriers or the reservation of fertility temporarily or permanently, allowing the other values of married intercourse to be preserved, are in some way against nature rather than a modification of behaviour to adapt natural outcomes to new conditions needs to be demonstrated. Even the strong opponents of change have agreed that the doctrine cannot be defended on the basis of reason alone. We can learn a great deal about how to respect our human natures from the physical elements of our being. It is important data but it must be weighed alongside other data. Even at the level of the human person as he has evolved there is far more to his totality than the physical aspects of his generative organs. By all means read his function from his form, but let it be his whole form – including his powers of reasoning, his psychological realities and his potentiality for recognizing the good. The onus of demonstrating the justification for elevating the physical aspect taken on its own into an unconditional moral value lies with those who propose the doctrine.

I am aware that a number of theologians would regard the points made above as irrelevant. They have replaced the biological model with the 'personalist' model. This, briefly, means that the moral quality of an act is primarily deduced from looking at how it is or is not consonant with the human person seeking to develop himself through a loving relationship. In such a model the balance between the use of sexuality for procreation and for the exclusive expression of love is a matter of judgement informed by virtue. I have no difficulty with this model provided that the entity we are concerned with is the whole human being, with due weight being given to his physical as well as to his spiritual aspects. That is, to treat the unitive purpose of sexual intercourse as merely incidental to its procreative purpose is no more questionable than to treat its procreative purpose as merely incidental to its unitive purpose. Neither purpose is absolute, neither purpose can be left out of account. I am aware that not giving an automatic primacy to one of these purposes creates an ambivalence between them. But I am comfortable with that – most of human life survives by coping with values which are in tension.

This 'whole human being' approach would confirm that the marriage act, while potentially profoundly expressing and confirming the bond between the couple, was equally ordered to procreation. Conceiving and raising children in a spirit of generous openness to life, rather than with a materialist focus on the selfish wants of the couple, would be seen as a privilege through which we are able to be agents of God's creative power. Larger rather than smaller families would be seen as the preferential option. The couple would do this responsibly taking into account the good of all concerned, including the needs of society, and would use the method of planning their family which best achieved these ends. One would assume that those who report that using safe period methods enhances their loving sexual expression would continue. Those who found that artificial barriers or reservation of fertility was a greater service to love would follow that route.[10] *Mutatis mutandis,* the sexual function was made for man, not man for the sexual function.

Dream on! you might respond. Yes, I do dream that this balanced view would be credible and indeed attractive to all those who sought their fulfilment as Christians through the married state. It might even succeed in countering the anti-life mentality which seems such a feature of Western society. Europe, at the Millennium, had a TFR of 1.4. Catholic Malta scores 1.7, equalling the UK, and Catholic Ireland scores 1.9, equalling France. Italy manages 1.3 and Spain, 1.2. Would a deeper understanding of sexuality on the part of the

Magisterium make it easier for good Catholics to hear the voice of the Church as the champion for life against a materialist and moribund society? Would the admirable expression of the Council's belief about conjugal love be freed from its shackles to inspire both the Church and the world?[11]

I have suggested that this is a doctrine in the process of transition. This implies that one position may gradually evolve into another. But in this case it cannot happen that way. By definition an absolutist position cannot evolve. It can either be held or it can be abandoned. I cannot say whether the doctrine will change at an official level although the belief and practice of the laity, so valued by Cardinal Newman, may well be witnessing to a truth of Christian living to which the Magisterium should be carefully attending. Certainly Catholics can and do form their consciences with regard to these and other issues. But the official position continues to affect many who do not have the confidence to make up their own minds; it affects the Church's international charity work; and it creates moral absurdities such as forbidding artificial insemination by husbands, or the use of condoms in countries where Aids is endemic.[12] It is not always enough to live quietly by one's own counsel – sometimes the prophetic voice of dissent is required.

It has been vehemently argued that a change in the Magisterium's doctrine on this issue would cause scandal, horrify those who have been faithful to the traditional teaching, and effectively destroy the basis of the Church's authority. This is always a danger when an organization has invested so much in her authority and consistency. Had she explicitly recognized that in many areas she could only give the best guidance available in the light of her current understanding the difficulty would not arise. But there are times when a bullet has to be bitten, not simply because accepting the provisional nature of the Church's moral understanding has to be faced up to at some time, and facing up to it now would at least limit the damage, but simply because it is true.

Notes to Appendix

1. A good summary of the history and the moral principles of this is given in a submission to the House of Lords concerning the sanctity of the embryo. *Tablet* (23 June 2001).
2. *Summa Theologica* I 92 1ad 1. Aquinas bases this on faulty biology, but he is clear that God's creative plan included women. Historical, theological and legal attitudes to women are documented at www.womenpriests.org.
3. *Summa Theologica Moralis* Vol. III, n. 465.
4. 'It may come as a surprise to physicians that theologians should have any difficulty about mutilations and other procedures which are performed with the consent of the subject but which have as their purpose the helping of others. By a sort of instinctive judgment we consider that the giving of a part of one's body to help a sick man is not only morally justifiable, but, in some instances, actually heroic.' Gerald Kelly, in *Theological Studies* 17 (1956), pp. 322–44.
5. The apparent exception of a woman defending her fertility against the invasion of the seed of a rapist has no force because she is not a volunteer and therefore she is not taking part in a human act. Similarly a spouse whose partner insists on using a barrier contraceptive may participate in the act while disapproving of this aspect.
6. *Summa Theologica* II II 154, 12.
7. *Casti Connubii* (1930), 59.
8. 1800 to 1980 data, R. Gill, N. Glazer and S. Thernstrom, *Our Changing Population* (Prentice-Hall 1992); 1990 data from US Bureau of the Census. I have taken the TFRs from the histogram on http://www.familydiscussions.com/charts/total–fertility.htm.
9. http://www.prb.org/Content/NavigationMenu–Other–reports/2000–2002/sheet2.html gives figures by world, region and country. Data provided by the Population Reference Bureau. The social realities which lie behind the statistics are frightening.
10. The survey evidence given to the Pontifical Commission on birth control by the Christian Family Movement showed that in

many instances the use of the safe period had a negative effect on married love and gave sexual activity an unhealthy prominence in the conduct of the marriage.

11. *Gaudium et Spes,* 49ff.

12. I am aware that condoms are by no means a panacea for Aids transmission – there are serious problems with user-failure. Better sexual morality, and of course the availability of modern drugs, are the long-term answer. But it is the view of disinterested experts that the use of condoms could, in the short – and practical – term, save many adult and infant lives. See for instance the 2001 report from the National Institute of Allergy and Infectious Diseases (www.niaid.nih.gov/dmid/stds/#5).However, even if condoms were 100 per cent effective against Aids transmission, the prohibition in its current terms would stand.

SELECT BIBLIOGRAPHY

Christian Ethics, an Introduction; Bernard Hoose (ed.), Continuum 2000.

Confronting the Truth, Conscience in the Catholic Tradition; Linda Hogan, Darton, Longman and Todd 2001

Conscience and its Right to Freedom; Eric D'Arcy, Sheed and Ward 1961

Contraception; John T. Noonan, Harvard University Press 1965

Embracing Sexuality, Authority and Experience in the Catholic Church; Joseph A. Selling (ed.), Ashgate 2001

Government and Authority in the Roman Catholic Church; Noel Timms and Kenneth Wilson, SPCK 2000

How to Get Your Own Way in Business; Quentin de la Bédoyère, Gower 1990

Managing People and Problems; Quentin de la Bédoyère, Gower 1989

Papal Sin, Structures of Deceit; Garry Wills, Darton Longman and Todd 2000

The Battle for the Catholic Mind; William E. May and Kenneth D. Whitehead (ed.), St Augustine's Press, 2001

The Catholic Moral Tradition Today, a Synthesis; Charles E. Curran, Georgetown University Press 1999

Themes in Fundamental Moral Theology; Charles E. Curran, University of Notre Dame Press 1977

The Reform of the Papacy, the Costly Call to Christian Unity; John R. Quinn, Crossroad 1999

INDEX